Existential Togetherness

Existential Togetherness

Toward a Common Black Religious Heritage

DeWayne R. Stallworth

FOREWORD BY
Lewis V. Baldwin

PICKWICK *Publications* · Eugene, Oregon

EXISTENTIAL TOGETHERNESS
Toward a Common Black Religious Heritage

Copyright © 2019 DeWayne R. Stallworth. All rights reserved. Except for brief quotations in critical publications or reviews, no part of this book may be reproduced in any manner without prior written permission from the publisher. Write: Permissions, Wipf and Stock Publishers, 199 W. 8th Ave., Suite 3, Eugene, OR 97401.

Cascade Books
An Imprint of Wipf and Stock Publishers
199 W. 8th Ave., Suite 3
Eugene, OR 97401

www.wipfandstock.com

PAPERBACK ISBN: 978-1-5326-5161-8
HARDCOVER ISBN: 978-1-5326-5162-5
EBOOK ISBN: 978-1-5326-5163-2

Cataloging-in-Publication data:

Names: Stallworth, DeWayne R., author. | Baldwin, Lewis V., foreword.

Title: Existential togetherness : toward a common Black religious heritage / DeWayne R. Stallworth ; foreword by Lewis V. Baldwin.

Description: Eugene, OR: Pickwick Publications, 2019. | Includes bibliographical references and index.

Identifiers: ISBN: 978-1-5326-5161-8 (paperback). | ISBN: 978-1-5326-5162-5 (hardcover). | ISBN: 978-1-5326-5163-2 (ebook).

Subjects: LCSH: African Americans—Religious life. | Black theology.

Classification: BR563.N4 S77 2019 (paperback). | BR563 (ebook).

Manufactured in the U.S.A.   AUGUST 2, 2019

This book is dedicated to the ancestors who survived the horrific trek of the Middle Passage. They embodied a degree of strength and fortitude that I can only capture in imagination. They survived together. We will thrive together.

Contents

Foreword by Lewis V. Baldwin | ix
Acknowledgments | xiii
Introduction | xv

1. An Existential Question of Worth | 1

2. Togetherness, Modernity, and Acculturation | 13

3. Trauma, Conversion, and the Mythical Meaning of the Slave Preacher | 52

Excursus: Du Bois, Racism, and Black Religion | 92

4. Martin Luther King Jr. and the Rhetoric of Existential Togetherness | 103

Epilogue: Black Privilege—The Antithesis to Existential Togetherness | 137

Bibliography | 143
Index | 153

Foreword

THE HISTORY AND CULTURE of African Americans have been viewed and treated over time through a range of interpretive frameworks. Cultural critics, historians, sociologists, anthropologists, economists, political scientists, psychologists, ethicists, and theologians have all made rich and enduring contributions, highlighting those themes that define and explain the black experience as it has unfolded from Africa to America. This wonderful book adds yet another chapter to this complicated and advancing folk saga.

Existential togetherness is the central theme coursing throughout the content of this important volume. DeWayne Stallworth skillfully uses it to frame a panoramic view of the black experience in the United States. This theme is quite significant in an historical, cultural, and spiritual sense, for it implies a lot in terms of the black experience as a *lived reality*, and also concerning how African Americans have viewed themselves, their experiences, and their relationship with one another and the world around them throughout the ages. For Stallworth, *existential togetherness* affords a conceptual and/or theoretical framework for tying together the different periods in the long history of African peoples in this country. The underlying point is that African Americans are a part of an unbroken history, or an experience that has historical continuity, particularly when considered in light of *existential togetherness.*

Dr. Stallworth begins by raising a rather loaded phenomenological question: What does it mean to be black, religious, and American in the United States in the twenty-first century? Although this question arises out of a contemporary context, he answers by focusing a steady gaze on the whole history of peoples of African descent.

He also opens with a discussion of the approaches taken by both black and white scholars regarding the existential question of worth relative to African Americans, arguing that white scholars dominated how this question was raised and answered up to the beginning of the twentieth century. Convinced that existential—phenomenological questions about the experiences, values, and worldview of any people must be answered in a larger historical context, Stallworth then turns to African cosmology and religious traditions in targeting the roots of the *existential togetherness* theme. He tells us that the existential ideal of community, which is synonymous with *existential togetherness*, originated out of an African ethos and carried over into the value systems of slave cultures in the New World. This conclusion is consistent with the findings of several pioneer scholars such as W. E. B. Du Bois, Melville J. Herskovits, Gayraud S. Wilmore, and Albert J. Raboteau, who contend that one has to look to Africa in order to understand certain dimensions of the African American religious and cultural experience.

In explaining how the existential ideal of community survived slavery to become a central aspect of the African American ethos and worldview, Stallworth turns to the black preacher, whom James Weldon Johnson credited with giving African peoples from various tribes their first sense of solidarity in America. We are told that the preacher, from the brush harbors on the plantation up to the civil rights campaigns of Martin Luther King Jr. and beyond, have always been supreme embodiments of this principle of *existential togetherness*. Moreover, the preacher, a creative and pivotal figure in the culture, has, according to Dr. Stallworth, always figured prominently in preparing and enabling African Americans to live out the demands of the existential ideal of community. The historical period that separates the slave preacher from King is not particularly problematic in this volume. Far more important is the spiritual and cultural bond that connects King to the traditions of the slave preacher, and the ways in which the slave preacher and King exercised the kind of unifying influence that gave practical expression to the *existential togetherness* principle in the context of black life. Clearly, it is the black preacher, first and foremost, that led in bringing to vivid life the existential ideal of community. A different trend begins to unfold in terms of *existential togetherness*, as Stallworth shows, after the death of King and the ending of the protest phase of the civil rights movement he led.

In the epilogue of this book, Stallworth concludes that the rise of classism and stratified privilege in certain sectors of black communal life has led to an erosion of the power of *existential togetherness* as both a theoretical principle and a practical reality. He refers to *black discontinuity*, and

Foreword

contends that the emergence of individualism, materialism, and a more privileged class among African Americans, and not simply white privilege alone, accounts for the failure of African Americans to sustain the kind of *existential togetherness* that brought their ancestors through the horrors of the slave trade, generations of enslavement, and segregation. These claims stand on solid ground, especially in view of the continuing breakdown of every vestige of the extended family—the centerpiece of *existential togetherness* in Africa and during slavery and Jim Crow—in African American culture since the civil rights movement. This book comes at a critical time in the history of black America. With the resurgence of white supremacy and nationalism, and the rise of xenophobia and Islamophobia in the United States, one wonders what will happen to African Americans in the absence of a strong sense and spirit of *existential togetherness*. In order to answer this question, one might begin with a careful reading of this work. It reminds us that we must first study and learn from the past in order to adequately engage the realities of the present, and properly prepare for the uncertainties of the future.

Lewis V. Baldwin
Emeritus Professor of Religious Studies
Vanderbilt University

Acknowledgments

MY NOTION OF EXISTENTIAL *togetherness* is birthed out of both lived experience and theory. First, I am a bona fide product of the *Black Church*. Experiencing the death of my mother at the age of five, and missing the presence of a father who was both physically and spiritually absent, I began seeking meaning and purpose early in life. I attempted to locate God within the context of my lived experience of suffering, but to no avail. As articulated in *Stable Conscience*,[1] a Baptist pastor, a man who is not my blood relative, decided to take me into his home and raise me as if I were is *flesh, blood, and bones*. To my recollection, this demonstration of charity and goodwill was my first experience of sensing the move of God in my life. It was through the actions of God's representative, the preacher, that I finally developed a sense of worth. Due to this experience, my notion of blackness, community, and church became inextricably blurred. I could no longer engage life without considering the oneness of this triune phenomenon. I, therefore, learned to interpret black communal progression within the context of black religious activism. Theoretically, if the black church/community, which is comprised of black people from various backgrounds, is to progress in this life, I believe such a movement is to be led by religious leaders. The theoretical idea of *existential togetherness* was conceptualized while matriculating as a graduate student at The Chicago Theological Seminary. I first attempted to treat this issue of *existential togetherness* in a thesis titled *Common religious heritage: ingenuity, enslavement, and the African ideal of existential togetherness*. I would like to thank Drs. Bo Myung Seo and Ken Stone, faculty members who sat on my defense committee, for encouraging me to expand this work into book form.

---

1. Stallworth, *Stable Conscience*, 13–19.

Acknowledgments

I would like to thank my American Baptist College family. The *Holy Hill* afforded me the opportunity to present my existential thoughts regarding African American religion in lectures, panel discussions, and collegial engagements. In particular, I would like to thank President Forrest E. Harris and Provost Lashante Walker for granting support throughout the writing process. I would also like to thank my colleague, Dr. Febbie Dickerson, for patiently listening to me think through much of this material.

Thanks are certainly due to my mentor, Dr. Lewis V. Baldwin, for his guidance throughout this laborious process. He has been especially helpful in the collection of source material for the King chapter, for which I am eternally grateful. As a (former) student of his, I have read essentially everything that Dr. Baldwin has published on the life and work of Martin Luther King Jr. He, nevertheless, continually proved his erudition regarding slave culture, black religion, and King scholarship through recommendations regarding the need for this work to display a type of *correlative analysis*. Additionally, our *think sessions* were most beneficial as they provided an interpretive guide for the construction and expansion of several sections in this volume. Dr. Baldwin's groundbreaking work, *There is a Balm in Gilead*, is an invaluable reference regarding the significance of King's cultural roots within the black church tradition. He is the first King scholar to expand the notion that the *Black Church*, in particular Ebenezer Baptist Church, provided meaning, purpose, and educational direction for King prior to his engagement with western modes of scholarship. Locating King's notion of worth and intellectual prowess in black culture is a pivotal component to the current scholarship that is presented in this volume.

Introduction

African American religious experience and particularly the experience of existential togetherness is ripe for phenomenological analysis, for while that experience is multifaceted it has not yet been explored or interpreted in sufficient depth. The word phenomenon derives from the Greek *phaenesthai*, to appear or emerge.[1] Reflection on phenomena as they are experienced leads toward an unbiased presentation of truth, in this case the truth of African American religious experience. Pure phenomenology, as developed in the mind and practice of Edmund Husserl,[2] examines "various strata of experience until one reaches something rock bottom and fundamental."[3] The goal of his philosophical notion of essential description is to elucidate essences of a given phenomenon. These individual essences, or subworlds,[4] are located in what Husserl defined as The *Lebenswelt*[5] (Everyday Life-World), in our case, the Everyday Life-World of African Americans. Maurice Merleau-Ponty in *Phenomenology of Perception*[6] understands the experience of freedom to entail this *Lebenswelt*, in which existential reflection is of the utmost concern. One cannot truly loathe or detest an experience until such an experience is known as it is experienced in anonymous flux. This location of consciousness provides a means by which the individual understands the human condition in a multi-varied context. For instance, the enslaved had the burden of ascertaining the meaning of being enslaved as well as interpreting how such an experience was to coincide

---

1. Moustakas, *Phenomenological Research Methods*, 26.
2. Brockelman, *Existential Phenomenology*, 27.
3. Ibid., 30.
4. Jung, ed., *Existential*, xx.
5. Ibid., xix.
6. Merleau-Ponty, "Freedom," 233.

with the existence of the slave owner. The merging of these two realities determined how freedom was to be interpreted existentially. Existential phenomenology, then, deviates from pure phenomenology by "uniting an extreme subjectivism with equally extreme objectivism by means of a reflective analysis of our everyday experience-in-the-world."[7] The whole is interpreted by its parts; devoid of presupposition, existential phenomenology observes the personal construction of reality within the Everyday-Life World, but it rejects the Husserlian ideal of objective evaluation in getting back in a pure sense to the *things themselves*. Yet being able to understand truth in one realm invariably increases the probability of understanding truth in the other, thereby creating an experience in which consciousness is observable in its fullest capacity.

How then to understand the African American religious experience? Many before me have tried. In *Honoring the Ancestors*, Donald Matthews structured his methodological approach to capture its essence. He sought to "understand what the black religious community already knows yet is constrained from affirming."[8] He took as an example of such constraint Benjamin E. Mays's *The Negro's God as Reflected in His Literature*, which, he said, was dualistic, and a nondialectical interpretation—meaning that Mays located the African American fight for social equity within a westernized interpretation of Christian orthodoxy. Rather than expand his method to include historical consideration for African influence, Mays "chose a mode of discourse which itself reflects a Western bias that favors literate over narrative means of expression. This method of analysis," noted Matthews, "led black theologians to overlook the narrative-based meanings of African American Christians."[9] Matthews' dialectical examination of the slave spiritual helped us to understand more accurately the depth and functionality of this cultural phenomenon, which he said defined the essence of the black religious community. Likewise, in *Dark Symbols, Obscure Signs*, Riggins Earl employed a hermeneutical phenomenology to construct what he terms *conversion-story language*.[10] His methodological approach was designed to understand: 1) slave masters' biblical hermeneutic, and 2) how slaves reconstructed the teachings that resulted from the masters' biblical hermeneutic. Yet as helpful as it was, Earl's work did not focus on

---

7. Brockelman, *Existential Phenomenology*, 52.
8. Matthews, *Honoring the Ancestors*, viii.
9. Ibid., 11.
10. Earl, *Dark Symbols, Obscure Signs*, 3.

Introduction

phenomena that highlighted the continuity between African American slave beliefs, practices of Christianity, and their origin in the African worldview. Focusing on the historical nexus of the African American experience provides an understanding regarding how some practices provide existential meaning within their Everyday Life-World.

In analyzing African funeral practices, for instance, Sterling Stuckey posits that "circular lines are formed as clockwise movements when linked to women, but are counter-clockwise motion sequences when employed for men."[11] This historical correlation of culture is a representation of existential themes, which Stuckey also defines as *togetherness and containment*.[12] The physical movement, says Stuckey, is the result of an African psychic norm that provides communal structure and cultural meaning to their civilization. Leonard E. Barrett posits that "it is important to note the homogeneity of the Blacks who came to the New World (despite their differences) in order to understand how they were able to interact effectively in their environment. Much has been made of their differences, but very little has been said of their similarity."[13]

To bridge this gap in African American religious studies, we need a broader understanding of togetherness in the lived experience of individuals with cultural connections to ingenuity, enslavement, and the African ideal of communal heritage. My existential phenomenological approach attempts to get at the essence of existential togetherness of African American lived experiences. I expand the notion of a common religious heritage by locating certain *togetherness* themes within the historical experience of the African American *Lebenswelt* (i.e., their Everyday Life-World) but beyond the slave and post-slavery literature, looking at pre-slavery contexts of African notions of community and togetherness. The interrelated realities of Everyday Life-World entails past, present, and future horizons. They are separate; yet, they are shared aspects of awareness which present a certain type of grouped consciousness. As a means of uncovering certain elements that present existence both subjectively and objectively, William Earle argues that "the essence of memory is therefore located in the relationship between two acts of consciousness, one present and one past; and, descriptively, what more can be said but that I am simply aware that I was

---

11. Stuckey, *Slave Culture*, 13.
12. Ibid.
13. Barrett, *Soul-Force*, 14.

Introduction

aware of something before."[14] Additionally, Sterling Stuckey contends, "that (lingering) memory enabled [African Americans] to go back to the sense of community in the traditional African setting and to include all Africans in their common experience of oppression in North America."[15] As a means of constructing a holistic perspective of the African American religious experience, this phenomenological analysis of historical memory for the African American involves examining existence within pre-slavery, slavery, and post-slavery thought.

With this in mind, my claim is twofold: First, that although those profiting from the American slave trade attempted to eradicate any and all vestiges of culture from the African enslaved psyche, slaves nevertheless maintained certain elements of their religious experiences and traditions; and because religion is experienced in every facet of African cultural expression, attempting to vanquish such expressions did not annihilate the continuation and practice of a common religious heritage as seen in existential togetherness. Indeed, enslavement actually enhanced the realization of such a phenomenon; it created the reality of existential togetherness for the enslaved African.

Second, I claim that the black church[16] is birthed out of the African communal idea of existential togetherness, which included a reverence for sacred space. Being connected to tribe, clan, and land held religious meaning for the enslaved African American. For instance, the African phrase *Ubuntu*[17] expresses the existential reality of a part being identified as a significant portion of the whole. The whole is devoid of purpose without the inclusion of unit parts. This type of religious identification is defined as a communal religious heritage. I contend, therefore, that the twenty-first century black church (i.e., community) should exhibit togetherness. It is these two notions of existential togetherness—the maintenance of both

14. Earle, *The Autobiographical Consciousness*, 142–74.

15. Stuckey, *Slave Culture*, 1.

16. I define the *Black Church* within the context of theorizing the notion of existential togetherness. The black church is not a monolithic phenomenon. It has many variations and complexities. It is, however, an extension of slave religion, which birthed a sense of community within oppressed African Americans in the diaspora. Whether an African American is Baptist, Methodist, Catholic, Presbyterian, Holiness, Agnostic, or Atheist, the fact remains that there is an unbroken bond that was created the moment the first shackles were placed on the body of the African. It is this heritage that I speak of when referring to the *Black Church*.

17. See Battle, *Reconciliation*, 35–53 and Lee, *We Will Get to the Promised Land*, 26–31.

INTRODUCTION

of elements of African religious practice and of a strong sense of community—that I explore in what follows.

Through this exploration, I hope to help fill the gap in current African American religious studies scholarship regarding notions of phenomenological correlation as seen in existential togetherness. By focusing on a particular phenomenon that is situated in black historical memory but has yet to appear in thematic fashion, I aim to present historical/cultural correlations between African ideals of community and the adapted version of this phenomenon expressed in the heritage of the American institution of slavery.

Four chapters present these correlations. Chapter 1 observes how scholars, both black and white, wrote about the existential question of worth for African American existence. I argue that this question was dominated by white scholars until the beginning of the twentieth century, when black scholars, such as W. E. B. Du Bois, began to publish scholarship presenting a very different notion of black worth.

Chapter 2 introduces the historical underpinnings of existential togetherness as seen as in African religious traditions. I illuminate African cosmology to understand the essence of the African experience —axiological order and cosmological structure. The existential ideal of community is a central theme within the African ethos; without it, cosmic intentionality is damaged, thus creating a context of meaninglessness. This chapter also focuses on the experience of European exploration, religious belief, notions of conquest, and African cultural negotiation. The beginning of modernity and the end of feudalism marked a turning point in which African peoples were identified as expendable commodities of labor. The structure of this European New World developed a system of high profitability. Certainly some risks were involved, but the risks were minimal in terms of the potential profits associated with the Atlantic slave trade. This chapter explores the trajectory of this European expansion, and how that expansion influenced the construction of the African American religious experience.

Chapter 3 examines the process by which African mythology informed how the slave preacher appropriated myth to align with African notions of God, self, and others. It connects African priesthood, acculturated religious beliefs, and constructions of leadership within an oppressed world and notes that the slave preacher held much influence over the content of communal conversation. I suggest that symbolism was the center of understanding for the enslaved African American by raising two questions: 1) What aspect of the New World corresponded to African ways of existence?

2) How could such a translation improve the level of existence for the enslaved? It is in this particular location that existential meaning is enhanced, and a cultural phenomenon (in this case, folk preaching) becomes the language of liberation for the enslaved, which is hermeneutically illuminated via the slave preacher.

Chapter 4 examines the cultural transmission that Martin Luther King Jr. exhibited as the leader for the modern civil rights movement. I first locate rhetorical themes of existential togetherness, particularly in his last speech before being assassinated. I then analyze ways in which the heroic depiction of King aligns with the traditional heritage of the African priesthood. I conclude that the heritage of existential togetherness is located in the psyche of a descendant of the slave preaching tradition, Martin Luther King Jr.

The epilogue examines the construction of the black racial class and stratified privilege. Although oppressed from systemic spaces of racism, some African Americans used their privilege to promote systemic spaces of inequality rather than annihilate them. This section also outlines the development of black discontinuity, and how the continuation of black privilege, not white privilege alone, has hindered the furtherance and wellbeing of the African American community.

1

A Question of Existential Worth

WHAT DOES IT MEAN to be black, religious, and American in the twenty-first century United States?[1] Blackness lends itself to various cultural/historical misrepresentations, so it is particularly important to examine the African American experience through a variety of disciplines.

The field of history, for instance, provides a framework from which to analyze factors that have defined black existence through various moments within historical time. Psychological scholarship furthers understanding of how the process of enslavement created a shift within the African psyche. Carter G. Woodson contends that any analysis of the African American experience must entail a process of integration consisting primarily of an historio-psycho approach.[2] The arena of religious studies is also important as religious belief is at the very core of what it means to exist as African. Anthropology and sociology illuminate the degree to which African Americans exist within highly defined social constructs. Such interdisciplinary methods of thinking through the African American experience helpfully engage the many nuances of African American existence.

---

1. The question, "What does it mean to be black and Christian?" was first posed in 1992 by African American scholars at Vanderbilt University School of Divinity (see Kelly Miller Smith Institute, Inc. "What Does It Mean to Be Black and Christian?," 1993). Anthony Pinn poses a similar question. See Pinn, *Terror and Triumph*, xi. My intention by using the *twenty-first century* is to present an epistemological correlation regarding prehistorical elements that helped define the current raison d'être for African Americans as seen in existential togetherness.

2. Woodson, *The Mind of the Negro*, xxiii.

To be sure, even an interdisciplinary approach can at times struggle to understand how the experience of enslavement redefined religious meaning for both African and acculturated African American. Therefore, a brief overview of the ways in which both early black and white intellectuals treated the question of black worth lays the groundwork for our discussion. Though early European treatment of black worth, with its notions of white superiority, is entirely problematic, scholars nevertheless have used European cultural misrepresentations to affirm a sense of meaning and worth, which they did largely by presenting historically inaccurate accounts of the African American experience.

My intention is not to provide a historiography of African American religious experience but to offer one way to locate a particular pattern of cognitive essences among African Americans. Some of these essences, although fraught with dubious analytical reasoning, establish a base line of perception regarding race, existential meaning, and purpose for African Americans.

European Treatment of Black Worth

One of the earliest European traveler's accounts of the African experience is Antonio Malfante's *Memoir* (1447), which claims "blacks are incestuous, heathen and cannibals."[3] This misrepresentation of Africans for centuries heavily informed how peoples of the world would come to view the continent and its inhabitants. With such racial bias and preconceived notions regarding the *other*, Europeans embarked upon a religiously motivated venture to dominate the world at the expense of an enslaved African workforce, humans they considered dispensable. David Brion Davis notes that Europeans' perception of "the Negro's cultural difference commonly served as the justification for his enslavement, reinforcing the myth that he had been rescued from heathen darkness and taken to a land of spiritual light."[4]

This so-called spiritual light led Europeans to inflict unfathomable horror upon African people for over four hundred years. Considering the moral conundrum of a religiously justified institution of slavery, Europeans busied themselves with the burdensome task of making arguments for anti-slavery and pro-slavery thought. Clergy of both factions rationalized their arguments on the basis of Christian scripture. Although the Puritans

---

3. Davidson, *The African Slave Trade*, 24.
4. Davis, *The Problem of Slavery*, 47.

sought to eradicate the physical abuses of slavery, they did not go far enough in addressing the dysfunctional system of slavery itself. Though in 1682, William Penn in *Articles of the Free Society of Traders* recommended that the "Negro slaves should be set free after serving a period of fourteen years,"[5] contrary to Penn's pronouncement of amelioration the Quakers[6] engaged in rhetorical hypocrisy, as many of them continued to own slaves. In 1701, Samuel Sewell sought to remedy such blatant contradictions associated with Quakerism. His pamphlet, "*The Selling of Joseph, A Memorial,* was widely distributed and influenced the progress of the early anti-slavery movement in other parts of the colonies."[7] William Sumner Jenkins contends that John Saffin's response to Sewell is the "first written defense of slavery in American history."[8] The debate between Sewell (anti-slavery) and Saffin (pro-slavery) fleshed out the diametrically opposed views in such a way that they could be disseminated verbatim. The published debate shows that both sides produced carefully constructed arguments.

Shortly after this, Cotton Mather's *Magnalia Christi Americana* (1702) glorified English Atlantic expeditions by reiterating the fact "that one main End of all these [Undertakings] was to plant the Gospel in these dark Regions of America."[9] Mather, a Puritan slave-owner and pastor, also published *The Negro Christianized* (1706) as a means of informing his colleagues of their moral obligation to educate their slaves in the traditions and customs of the Christian faith. In 1710, Mather then published his *Essays to Do Good*, which urged slave masters and mistresses to take better care of their slaves because, argued Mather, God had created the state of slavery to redeem the heart of the pagan African. Mather's goal of improving the institution of slavery via Christian instruction further enhanced the prevalent notion that Europeans were divine agents and that the institution of slavery was a means by which the inferior African was privileged to learn that the Christian God was the creator of their savage souls.

---

5. Jenkins, *Pro-Slavery Thought in the Old South*, 7.

6. George Fox was the founder of The Society of Friends (also known as the Quakers). Fox et al., began their anti-slavery protestations in the middle of the seventeenth century. Ralph Sandiford, Benjamin Lay, John Woolman, and Warner Mifflin are several adherents of the Society to affect change between the years 1640 and 1754. Sobel contends that the aforementioned utilized dream analysis to better understand their complicity with a system that they verbally and fraternally denounced. See Sobel, *Teach Me Dreams*, 62–65.

7. Ibid., 4.

8. Ibid.

9. See Mather, *Magnalia Christi Americana*, vol. 1, book 1, ch. 1.

> Oh! That the souls of our slaves were of more account with us! That we gave a better demonstration that we despise not our own souls, by doing what we can for the souls of our slaves, and not using them as if they had no souls! . . . Methinks, common principles of gratitude should incline you to study the happiness of those, by whose obsequious labors your lives are so much accommodated. Certainly, they would be the better servants to you, the more faithful, the more honest, the more industrious, and submissive servants to you, for your bringing them into the service of your common Lord.[10]

Yet Mather's contention about the probable soul equity/equality of the slave was problematic for slave owners. Ironically, his interpretation of religion would be used by anti-slavery advocates to further the notion that soul identification presupposed the essence of slaves' humanity. Conversely, the slave masters argued that the slave had no soul, and that the slave was of a different species; therefore, Christianity was useless. The debate over slaves' participation in the sacraments, for example, was therefore rejected based on the social implications of slaves worshipping together with slave masters.

The Rev. C.C. Jones' book *The Religious Instruction of the Negroes in the United States* published in 1842 reiterated Mather's advice about soul equality and the need to instruct slaves in Christianity.[11] It provides us with a lens through which to observe early missionary efforts "among the slaves prior to the nineteenth century."[12]

Understandably, the idea of spiritual equality prompted some blacks to embrace other expressions of equality, such as dress and European cultural respectability. Dr. Holocombie praises Andrew Bryan, a black early nineteenth-century Baptist minister and slave owner,[13] for his uncanny negation of African heritage for that of a better acceptable European representation:

---

10. Jenkins, *Pro-Slavery Thought in the Old South*, 15–16.

11. Harrison, *Gospel Among the Slaves*, 38.

12. Within this period Jones failed to make mention of the religious slave meetings that were conducted outside the supervision of white slave owners. House slaves were, to a certain degree, privileged. Within the demoralizing state of being property for sale, the house slaves lived in conditions similar to their respective owners. Additionally, they were allowed to be present when the white family received religious instruction. This cultural division of the slaves presented a construction of stratification, which in turn influenced the development of certain animosities within the slave community. See Harrison, *Gospel Among the Slaves*, 38.

13. Bryan, "A Letter from the Negro Baptist Church in Savannah," 49–51. According to Carter G. Woodson, Andrew Bryan, before 1790, was an established slave master in

A Question of Existential Worth

> Andrew Bryan has, long ago, not only honorably obtained liberty, but a handsome estate. His fleecy and well-set locks have been bleached by eighty winters; and, dressed like a Bishop of London, he rides, moderately corpulent, in his chair, and with manly features, of a jetty hue, fills every person to whom he gracefully bows with pleasure and veneration, by displaying in smiles even rows of natural teeth, as white as ivory, and a pair of fine black eyes, sparkling with intelligence, benevolence, and joy. In giving daily thanks to god for his mercies, my aged friend seldom forgets to mention the favorable change that has of late years appeared through the lower parts of Georgia, as well as of South Carolina, in the treatment of servants.[14]

Certainly some blacks like Andrew Bryan gained a sense of acceptance through obtaining white societal accoutrements. We see this also in an earlier era between curious Africans and opportunistic European explorers. For instance, Esteban Montejo remembers that the cause of his enslavement was a direct result of Africans being enticed by European goods. This desire only increased with time. When some African rulers ran out of captured prisoners to sell to Europeans, they began to sell members of their own communities as a means to appease their desire for European possessions.[15] William Edward Burghardt Du Bois describes a similar situation in which "Hamed Muhammed, a [n]egro, better known as Tippoo-Tib, was one of the greatest of slave traders. He eventually became a sultan and overlord of the country of Kassongo in the very middle of central Africa, which he made a center of ivory collecting and slave hunting. He had a thousand muzzle-loading guns. And it was not until 1905 that he died."[16] Additionally, Africans fought other African peoples as a means of escaping the prospect of slavery. Captured Africans had to fight Europeans on the slave ships as well as in the strategically stationed baracoons[17]— the prison cells created to house hordes of African peoples.[18] In 1927, Zora Neale Hur-

Savannah, Georgia. See Woodson, *The Negro in Our History*, 39.

14. Jones, *The Religious Instruction*, 52.
15. Rodney, *How Europe Underdeveloped Africa*, 79.
16. Du Bois, *The World and Africa*, 60.
17. Sylviane A. Diouf's work addresses ways in which West African peoples strategically responded to the aggressive pursuit of both African and European slave traders. African response was seen in defensive strategies, protective strategies, and offensive strategies. See Diouf, *Fighting the Slave Trade*.
18. We can think of this as the beginning of what is known in the twenty-first century as mass incarceration.

ston, while interviewing Cudjo Lewis, the last living African who had experienced capture, enslavement, and freedom, reported him as saying that

> We stay dere in de barracoon three weeks. We see many ships in de sea, but we cain see good cause de white house, it tween us and de sea. But Cudjo see de white men, and dass somethin' he ain' never seen befo'. In de Takkoi we hear de talk about de white man, but he doan come dere. De barracoon we in ain' de only slave pen at the place. Dey got plenty of dem but we doan know who de people in de other pens. Soetime we holler back and forth and find out where each other come from. But each nation in a barracoon by itself. We not so sad now, and we all young folks so we play game and clam up de side de barracoon so we see whut goin' on outside. When we dere three weeks a white man come in de barracoon wid two men of de Dahomey. One man, he a chief of Dahomey and de udder one his word-changer. Dey make everybody stand in a ring—'bout ten folkses in each ring. De men by dey self, de women by dey self. Den de white man lookee and lookee. He lookee hard at de skin and de feet and de legs and in de mouth. Den he choose. Every time he choose a man he choose a woman. Every time he take a woman he take a man, too. Derefore, you unnerstand me, he take one hunnard thiry. Sixty-five men wid a woman for each man. Dass right. Den de white man go way. I think he go back in de white house. But de people of Dahomey come bring us lot of grub for us to eatee cause dey say we goin' leave dere. We eatee de big feast. Den we cry, we sad' cause we doan want to leave the rest of our people in de barracoon. We all lonesome for our home. We doan know whut goin' become of us, we doan want to be put apart from one another.[19]

Until people like Hurston started reporting such information, for nearly six centuries, European thought regarding the experience of African Americans was invariably influenced by racial bias.[20] Consequently, African Americans have been viewed as animals/non-human/sub-human.[21]

---

19. Hurston, *Barracoon*, 53–54.

20. Long, *Significations*, 194.

21. The act of dehumanization diminishes worth and replaces it with a void expression of existential meaninglessness. Jacques Derrida's work acknowledges the philosophical difference between the human and the *animal*. But what causes such a difference? Derrida raises the former question after looking at his cat (and allowing the cat to look back at him). Does God equate the existence of the human and the animal to be that of equal value? This type of questioning is beneficial to theological anthropology and religious studies. Derrida contends that human vulnerability negates hubris and condescension.

A QUESTION OF EXISTENTIAL WORTH

On this, Anthony Pinn asserts that slavery was a process in which roles were ontologically defined. The enslaved, for instance, were forced to subscribe to the social role of object, while the slave-master took on the social role of subject:

> Slavery's power lies in the eradication of Africans as subjects and the manner in which the enslaved African is re-created in the context of the New World as an object, depersonalized, a nonbeing. As such, enslaved Africans occupied a strange space in that they existed outside the recognized boundaries of human community while also being a necessary part of that same community—as a workforce and as the reality against which whiteness was defined. These factors, when combined with physical darkness, resulted in the state of social death that defines slavery and the slave. Slaves had the physical form of the human but because of their social death possessed none of the attributes, rights, and liberties associated with being human. How this status, or lack of status, was transferred to children born of slaves is also important here because, although the United States imported a small percentage of the New World's Africans, it was able to increase the number of slaves held through "breeding."[22]

Delineation should promote appreciation for the subjective distinction of both human and animal—both are God's special creation. Derrida's cat prompts him to consider the *what if's* of life? Can the cat *see* him; in all nakedness, walk into the bathroom? Does the cat speak; if so, what language? I appreciate Derrida's philosophical understanding of the animal within the works of notable scholars (i.e., Descartes, Kant, Heidegger, Lacan and Levinas); however, in the interest of applying Derrida's work to that of an hermeneutic of black bodies, I am not clear on whether the cat, or a black body, has a voice at the end of such an analysis. Metaphorically speaking, a family pet will always survive when pitted against a dehumanized object.

Certainly a theological anthropologist could provide an epistemological understanding as to why an animal's worth is tantamount to that of a human being; be that as it may, most lay persons would perhaps agree that it is standard ethical reasoning to save a human life over that of a family pet. Such was, and is, the case for individuals that are black, religious and American. One is left to ponder in Derridian fashion, is black life greater than that of an animal? See Derrida, *The Animal That Therefore I Am*.

22. Pinn, *Terror and Triumph*, 16. The projected animalistic nature upon African Americans is seen in the act of lynching. Arthur Raper asserts, "three thousand seven hundred and twenty-four people were lynched in the United States from 1889 through 1930. Over four-fifths of these were Negroes." Moreover, "On numerous occasions, there was no apparent reason for the lynching, no "crime" committed, no social norm discarded. The mere fact that the victims were black was enough." See, for example, Raper, *The Tragedy of Lynching*, 1. Also, see Patterson's treatment on slave dehumanization in *Slavery and Social Death* and Wells-Barnett 's, *On Lynchings*.

By the Revolutionary age, sympathetic whites began a campaign that built on Baxter and Mather's argument regarding the enslaved Africans' right and fight for freedom. Abolitionists argued that the declaration of equity and equality was an indisputable gift from God. They insisted that this language was found in the forms of rebellion against the British Crown such as The *United States Declaration of Independence*. Ironically, the very document that would free the colonists from tyranny also became the tool that eventually catalyzed the anti-slavery debate. The Revolutionary period also marked an increase of natural law rhetoric among the abolitionists.[23] Abolitionists saw a correlation between the *Declaration of Independence*'s rhetoric of *all men being created equal with the freedom to pursue life, liberty and happiness* with that of the slaves' request to be viewed as God's creation, with equal rights like any other human being, thus making natural law rhetoric the most successful tactic employed to combat pro-slavery thought.[24]

The *Declaration* was the principal document by which law was established across the land; regardless of the geographical location, the declaration of rights was to be applied to *all men*. The natural law argument also addressed the issue of morality. Religion had been used as a means to legitimate the notion of racism and enslavement. The natural law argument, however, afforded anti-slavery rhetoricians an opportunity to quell subversive attempts at legitimizing slavery as a religious mandate.[25]

African American Treatment of Black Worth

The spirit of social analysis penetrated well into the early twentieth century when highly educated African Americans began to present scholarly arguments against the racist European scholarship legitimizing a superior/inferior race division. By the end of the nineteenth century and beginning

23. Jenkins, *Pro-Slavery Thought in the South*, 33.
24. Ibid.
25. By articulating an inclusionary expansion of *all men*, Dr. Martin Luther King Jr. would strategically use the natural law argument to combat racism on legal grounds. Furthermore, this dichotomy of moral legality formed the basis from which African American leaders such as King would illuminate the rhetorical hypocrisy of America—King would aptly articulate in several speeches, "be true to what you (i.e., America) put on paper (i.e., *Declaration of Independence* and *The Constitution of the United States of America*)." King simply refused to argue a moral issue based on a religious hermeneutic alone.

of the twentieth century, several black scholars were articulating black significance as lived and experienced by black people.[26] Of these, George Washington Williams' was the first comprehensive historical account of the black race in America. Williams' *History of the Negro Race in America From 1619 to 1880. Vols. 1 and 2* (1882) was published in an era in which African Americans desperately needed to affirm their understanding of cultural significance. Williams' book paved the way for future black scholars to analyze the Negro problem from within the context of the religio-historical movement of a people.

Not long thereafter, in 1896 W. E. B. Du Bois, the first African American *religious* scholar, published his doctoral thesis, *The Suppression of the African Slave Trade, 1638–1870*, the same year in which the United States Supreme Court struck down notions of equity and equality for American Americans in *Plessy v. Ferguson*. Du Bois's dissertation critically considered the intricate institutional structure that so negatively affected the lives of millions of Africans. In his subsequent 1898 book *The Study of the Negro Problems*, Du Bois pivoted from the dissertation's historical and theoretical treatment of slavery to address specific problems that emerged due to the historical experience of slavery. Although he acknowledged several general historical experiences of the American Negro, he nevertheless insisted that an examination of the historical account is what promotes intellectual and practical lessons for the Negro scholar. From May 25 to 26, Du Bois led the Third Conference for the study of the Negro Problems. Operating in the capacity of secretary, Du Bois et al., subsequently published *Some Efforts of American Negroes For Their Own Social Betterment* (1898). This research illumined Du Bois' early treatment of the African American religious experience:

> It is natural that to-day the bulk of organized efforts of the Negroes in any direction should centre in the Church. The Negro Church

---

26. Rev. Alexander Crummell organized *The American Negro Academy* on March 5, 1897. Its Constitution reads in part: "The Academy is an organization of authors, scholars, artists and those distinguished in other walks of life, men of African descent, for the promotion of Letters, Science and Art; for the creation, as far as possible, of a form of intellectual taste, for the encouragement and the assistance of youthful but hesitant scholarship, for the stimulation of inventive and artistic powers, and for the promotion of the publication of works of merit." Membership consisted of scholars such as W. E. B. Du Bois, Francis J. Grimke, J. Albert Johnson, Kelly Miller, John L. Love, W.T.S. Jackson, Gabriel N. Grisham, Levi J. Coppin, R.R. Wright, Sr., Walter B. Hayson, Matthew Anderson, A.P. Miller, Lewis B. Moore, Charles C. Cook, William H. Ferris, W.S. Scarborough and John Cromwell. See Du Bois, *Papers (MS 312)*, 1917.

is the only social institution of the Negroes which started in the African forest and survived slavery; under the leadership of the priest and medicine man, afterward of the Christian pastor, the Church preserved in itself the remnants of the African tribal life and became after emancipation the centre of Negro social life. So that to-day the Negro population of the United States is virtually divided into Church congregations, which are the real units of the race life.[27]

In 1899 Du Bois further narrowed his academic scope by investigating the lived experience of *The Philadelphia Negro*, but broadened it once again in his 1903 book *Souls of Black Folk*, in which he illuminated every dimension of black life. His theory of *double consciousness* provided a framework from which one could understand contextually the psychological angst associated with existing as one person within two realities or worlds—the black and the white.

Expanding upon that work, in 1911 Alexander Francis Chamberlain's *The Contribution of the Negro to Human Civilization* addressed how sufferers of Angolsaxonism and Negrophobia failed to recognize the ingenuity of black people. Du Bois, in his 1915 book *The Negro* again presented black persons to the world as people of historical significance and sophistication. Benjamin G. Brawley's *A Social History of the American Negro* (1921) treated the problem of the Negro from a socio/historical paradigm. His work built upon Williams' (1882) work.[28] Carter G. Woodson's *The Negro in Our History* (1922) then presented a historical analysis of black people and their connection to a past filled with strength, honor, and ingenuity. Alaine Locke disavowed preconceived notions of Negro inferiority in his 1925 work *Harlem: Mecca of the New Negro*. Benjamin E. Mays' *The Negro's God, as reflected in his Literature* (1938) located God within the rhetoric of black folk, which furthered the notion that black people did indeed possess spiritual intelligence.

In 1939, E. Franklin Frazier attempted to address the historical continuity of blackness by examining the black family in the United States. In *The Negro Family in the United States,* he explained, however, that slavery and the process of dehumanization were too severe for the enslaved to bear; as a result, African familial patterns were destroyed. This emphasis only furthered a type of caricature of the enslaved black as submissive,

---

27. Du Bois, "The Study of the Negro Problems," 1–23.
28. Brawley, *A Social History of the American Negro*, ix.

A QUESTION OF EXISTENTIAL WORTH

unintelligent, and obedient. Although David Walker's *Appeal* (1829) was well known, as were the rebellious tactics of Nat Turner (1831), Denmark Vesey (1822) and Gabriel Prosser (1800), it was not until the publication of Herbert Aptheker's *American Negro Slave Revolts* (1943) that major thought went into academically refuting notions of the so-called Sambo slave personality. Contrary to the theory of slave acquiescence, Aptheker concluded that slave rebellions in fact commenced the moment Africans were forced into enslavement. Moreover, Melville J. Herskovits' *Myth of the Negro Past* (1941) challenged Frazier's notion of social annihilation. Herskovits also presented the notion that the *weak and submissive* black was a fallacy that was based on an illogical premise of black humans possessing genetically inferior DNA. Instead, Herskovits proved the cultural continuity between Africans and African Americans. John Hope Franklin's *From Slavery to Freedom* (1947) outlined a contextual history for blacks—one that entailed African tradition, cultural relevancy, religious ingenuity, and political power. E. Franklin Frazier's *The Negro Church in America* (1963) reiterated the sociological breakdown described in his earlier work, but *The Negro Church* outlined how Christianity severed any connection blacks had to Africanisms. Joseph Washington's *The Negro and Christianity in the United States* (1966) furthered the disillusionment regarding the superiority of white Christianity, and the lack of black theological acuity as it relates to the pursuit of the Christian God.

Thus, a century of scholarship contributed to the advancement of some positive regard for African American existence. The civil rights era, however, was a time in which black existence was vehemently challenged by the predominant praxis of white ideological supremacy. While blacks were murdered, tortured, and terrorized, scholars aggressively analyzed and studied the existential plight of the Negro experience. They sought to provide scholarship that set the black experience within a proper historical context. Since the civil rights era, scholars such as Leonard E. Barrett (*Soul-Force: African Heritage in Afro-American Religion*), John Blassingame (*The Slave Community*), Lerone Bennett (*Before the Mayflower*), Charles H. Long (*Significations: Signs, Symbols, and Images in the Interpretation of Religion*), Lawrence Levine (*Black Culture and Black Consciousness*), Milton Sernett (*African American Religious History: A Documentary Witness*), Albert Raboteau[29] (*Slave Religion: The "Invisible Institution" in the Antebellum*

---

29. Raboteau mentions how his thesis was misinterpreted by aligning his analysis with the thought of E. Franklin Frazier. He states in part: "Perhaps I could make clearer

South), Herbert Gutman (*The Black Family in Slavery and Freedom: 1750-1925*), Vincent Harding (*There is a River*), Peter Paris (*Spirituality of African Peoples*), Eugene D. Genovese (*Roll, Jordan, Roll*), Mechal Sobel (*Trabelin' On*), Kenneth M. Stamp (*The Peculiar Institution*), and Sterling Stuckey (*Slave Culture: Nationalist Theory and the Foundation of Black America*) built upon the established claim that African cultural heritage has indeed strongly influenced cultural expression within African American identity.[30] In other words, the essence of the African American religious experience is located in several equally important experiences. Getting to the core of such a multilayered experience requires an approach that emphasizes individual functions of a phenomenon as a means of uncovering the essence of its existence. For the African American, engaging an authentic existence entails understanding phenomenological nuances, which created the here-and-now reality of being African, American, and religious.

---

to those who have misinterpreted me as simply saying African religions disappeared in the United States that what I was attempting to say is that the distinctiveness of the slaves' religious culture lay not in their preservation of *Africanisms* but in the African perspectives, habits, preferences, aesthetics, and styles with which Africans and their American descendants shaped their religious choices in the very diverse situations and circumstances of slavery" (*Slave Religion*, 330).

30. Long also credits the following scholars for addressing the issue of African American religious interpretation: Benjamin E. Mays and Joseph W. Washington, *The Negro's Church* (New York: Russell and Russell, 1969); Arthur Fauset, *Black Gods in the Metropolis* (Philadelphia: University of Pennsylvania Press, 1944); Howard Brotz, *The Black Jews of Harlem* (New York: Schocken, 1970); C. Eric Lincoln, *The Black Muslims in America* (New York: Beacon, 1961); and E. U. Essien-Udom, *Black Nationalism: The Search for an Identity in America* (Chicago: University of Chicago Press, 1962). (Long, *Significations*, 197).

2

Existential Togetherness

Amid shouting's of panic, more and more toubob [white Europeans] scrambled to the scene, rushing out of doors and sliding like monkeys down from among the billowing white cloths. As the women shrieked, the shackled men huddled together in a circle. The metal sticks barked flame and smoke; then the big black barrel exploded with a thunderous roar and a gushing cloud of heat and smoke just over their head, and they screamed and sprawled over each other in horror.[1]

PRIOR TO THE EXPERIENCE of European enslavement, African existential meaning and purpose was based in a contextual understanding of clan and tribal affiliations. "Indeed," argues Raboteau, "it was only after they were brought to America that Africans began to think of themselves as just Africans, instead of Ibo, Akan, or Bakongo."[2] The predominant principle of social relations was that of family (i.e., kinship associated with communalism).[3] The concept of community was a central tenet in African cosmology. Although Africans approached life as an individualized experience, the acquisition of individual goals was validated only if those goals fit within the ethos of community enhancement. The community consisted of a contextualized structure of roles within a socio-religious pattern; for instance, "in the descending order of power from the supreme God, through

---

1. Haley, *Roots*, 177.
2. Raboteau, *Canaan Land*, 7.
3. Rodney, *How Europe Underdeveloped Africa*, 36.

the sub divinities, ancestral spirits, communal and familial leaders, to the youngest child, the highest good of each is the same, namely, the preservation and promotion of the community's well-being."[4] The European institution of slavery, however, challenged this sense of communal understanding and existence.

Europeans' enslavement of Africans had three phases. The first phase entailed small bands of men raiding small sections of the continent in sporadic movements. The second phase entailed proposing to African chiefs the exchange of European goods (chiefly horses, firearms, and alcohol) for humans, thus establishing a system of trade. The third phase entailed Mamdu, Lord of Mali, requesting Portuguese military assistance against his enemies. This invitation sparked a chain reaction of European involvement and influence of war among African tribes.[5] To combat the newly established influence of European military expansion, Queen Nzinga founded the Angolan state of Matamba in 1630:

> The formidable Nzinga continued war with peace terms imposed by Portugal. Nzinga subsequently allowed Capuchin priests to enter Matamba, and she cooperated in their efforts to convert her subjects. Among the most feared and powerful rulers in Africa, Queen Nzinga was apparently a sincere convert. As a condition for receiving the Catholic sacrament of communion, Nzinga gave up wearing traditional amulets dedicated to the ancestors or deities. At the age of seventy she reluctantly renounced polyandry and agreed to solemnize her union with a young man according to the rites of the Catholic Church, which united them in a permanent bond so that her subjects "should have no opportunity or excuse not to imitate her." In a pattern that would be replicated elsewhere in Africa where Christianity was state imposed, Nzinga exhorted her people to practice monogamy and have their children baptized on pain of exile and to abandon "diabolical relics" like horns and girdles and gourds dedicated to various deities in favor of Christian reliquaries. On Nzinga's orders Christian holy days such as Christmas and Easter were substituted for traditional festivals and the traditional paraphernalia of worship was either confiscated and burned or given to the missionaries for use in the Catholic liturgy. According to Father Giovanni Cavazzi, Nzinga "no longer honoured or revered the witch-doctors and sorcerers, but became

---

4. Paris, *Virtues and Values*, 5.
5. Davidson, *The African Slave Trade*, 101.

their enemy and persecutor," executing some, exiling and banishing others.[6]

This political and military movement, however, only slowed and did not end European expansion. The accustomed notions of African community were thus re-defined, as captured Africans learned to implement notions of togetherness in an oppressed and chaotic community of enslavement. Due to the multifaceted nature of the African continent, newly captured Africans had to overcome geographical, tribal, and national barriers in order to establish a common manner through which liberation could be universally communicated[7] —but to do so in a way that white slave traders could not understand. We see the great tradition of black protest[8] in African people's refusal to acquiesce to notions of inferiority and oppression. Notwithstanding language barriers, enslaved Africans used common African practices to secure a particular ethos of rebellion. One such practice is the use of drums. Because the use of drums was a practice of common religious heritage for African peoples, even when language differences between captured Africans made it difficult to communicate, the drums alerted conveyed messages to captured Africans about rebellions and so forth.[9]

As they traversed the Atlantic, the newly enslaved Africans no doubt cried out to God/Allah. Some Africans, upon seeing white men with guns, quickly grabbed sand and placed it in their mouths. Taking sand communicated that the individual was just as much a part of the land as the land was a part of the individual. Likewise, thoughts of Africa (e.g., of the trees, food, water, villages, hills, mountains, languages, tribes, animals, and sand) gave the newly enslaved hope that the prospect of returning home to the freedom of communal worship was a realistic goal. This was done as a means of keeping some part of their homeland with them as they traveled across the Atlantic to the New World.[10] The religious experience of the former substantiates the claim of African ritualistic practice.[11]

Africans viewed every element of human endeavor and cultural variation as religious. Although they believed the Supreme Being sustained

---

6. Frey and Wood, *Come Shouting to Zion*, 8–9.
7. Harding, *There is a River*, 4.
8. Ibid., 14.
9. Blassingame, *The Slave Community*, 22.
10. See Harding, *There Is a River*.
11. Long, *Significations*, 32.

every aspect of creation, Africans also believed that the lower deities (i.e., ancestors) continued to dwell within the kinship after death.[12] John Hope Franklin states that "there was veneration for spirits that dwelt on the family land, in the trees and rocks, throughout the community of the kinship group, and in the sky above the community."[13] The Supreme Being allotted meaning and purpose for every organism through the care of subordinate spiritual powers.[14] With this in mind, and their kidnapping from Africa, it is reasonable to ask whether newly enslaved Africans felt religiously disconnected from ancestral deities upon their departure from Africa.

The African religious heritage encompasses thousands of years of generational transmission.[15] Although such a religious experience cannot be traced back to its inception, it nevertheless was clearly an impressive tradition. The African ideals of God, land, culture, self, and others expressed orally do not imply that Africans were unable to express thoughts in written form;[16] just the opposite, isolation from different peoples of the world created a world in which oral tradition was as valuable as a written text. This oral transmission was an indelible part of the psyche of captured Africans, who would eventually give that transmission new religious meaning within an enslaved existence.

The ingenuity among the African enslaved caused grave concern for the slave traders and slave holders for feared uprisings and a loss of their power. They therefore sought to eradicate any form of togetherness among the enslaved. As Geoffrey Parrinder notes, "there were laws against the education of Africans, laws against the assembling of Africans. They outlawed many rituals connected with African religious practices, including dancing and the use of drums." Moreover, "in many places they banned African languages. Thus they attempted to shut black people out from both cultures, to make them wholly dependent"[17] Under the sanctioned institution of chattel slavery, the experience of African peoples in America was highlighted by existential moments of torture, trauma, and death. The former experiences affected the ways in which Africans began to re-examine their raison d'être.

---

12. Mbiti, *Introduction to African Religion*, 16.
13. Ibid., 25.
14. Franklin and Moss, *From Slavery to Freedom*, 24.
15. Ibid., 12.
16. Parrinder, *Religion in Africa*, 18.
17. Ibid., 27.

Existential Togetherness

Prior to their enslavement, Africans found meaning (and thus religious meaning) in every facet of human existence.[18] Although each African people had its own cultural heritage,[19] religious belief was at the very core of all African peoples' social and cultural understanding. John Mbiti notes that, "religion has been for Africans the normal way of looking at the world and experiencing life itself."[20] For the enslaved African, religion was experienced in the water, forest, sky, ground, community, and so on. Africans similarly understood community to be the central element in life; as Peter Paris states, "this means more than the maintenance of a symbiotic relation between the individual and the community."[21] But the process of enslavement and repeated separations from kinsfolk forced some blacks to disregard this heritage.

Phyllis Wheatley, touted as the first female African American poet in America, published a poem in 1773 titled *On Being Brought from Africa to America*[22] that echoed what Europeans were saying: that African religious experience was flawed in comparison to the more theologically advanced European understanding of the divine. This religious perspective added to the perception that slavery, although harsh in nature, was a means by which God providentially used the American institution of slavery to rescue the religiously uncouth African from pagan worship. The very religion that Wheatley praised was also appropriated to incite internal conflict among African tribes. With religion and gun, white men began to convince African leaders that slavery and violence were the ultimate answer to the problem of tribal conflict.

> Ancient political balances and structures of power and alliances were shattered through the introduction of Europe's firearms into the hands of one side or another. Often the arms were used as bribes to encourage leaders to capture men, women, and children from adjoining nations and tribes. Wars were declared for no other reason than to obtain prisoners. Villages were razed; hunting parties never returned home. Families and tribes, and centuries of traditions, were broken. And eventually the trails of the West African lands were beaten smooth by the bare feet of millions of our ancestors, as they made their way down to the rivers and the

18. Franklin and Moss, *From Slavery to Freedom*, 25.
19. Mbiti, *Introduction to African Religion*, 7.
20. Ibid., 12.
21. Paris, *The Spirituality of African Peoples*, 111.
22. Wheatley, "On Being Brought from Africa to America," 41.

sea. For a long time the Europeans, sustained by their guns and Bible, and by arrogance and cruelty, were convinced that all things white and Christian were possible.[23]

Although profiteers of the American slave trade attempted to eradicate any vestiges of their native culture from the African enslaved psyche,[24] slaves nevertheless maintained certain elements of their religious experiences and traditions. And because religion is experienced in every facet of African cultural expression, attempting to eliminate such expressions invariably influenced the practice of the common religious heritage of existential togetherness.

Within the context of this work, existential togetherness derives from the lived experience of the enslaved African (American). In order to approach this problem effectively, one must ascertain African meaning in regard to being stolen, ripped from one's country, land, and people, forced to work the rest of one's worldly days as chattel—i.e., as an animal, an object of zero worth, a commodity and as a legal possession— and most often separated from one's kindred. This new experience of chattel slavery separated a highly philosophical and religious people(s) from their cultural lands. That land, formerly liberated space but now invaded and plundered, allowed Africans to experience God through interaction within the community, tribe, and clan. African scholars like Geoffrey Parrinder, John Mbiti, and Basil Davidson agree about the importance of kinship within the African familial unit. For example, take Mbiti's notion of the importance of genealogical awareness of kinship. Knowing one's historical provenance and predecessors typically promotes a sense of pride and self-worth, and certainly of identity. Being connected to individuals in a clan provided existential certainty of purpose, meaning, and identity. One was the clan, and the clan became such a one. "Clans are normally totemic," argues Mbiti, "the totem is the visible symbol of unity, of kinship, of belonging, of togetherness and common affinity."[25] Slavery abruptly and brutally disrupted and modified the existential structure of clan and tribal togetherness. It is reasonable to wonder whether there was as a result a sense of communal survival within the enslaved community.

Religion has always been at the core of African peoples' cultural experience and identity; for many, being African meant having a communal

---

23. Harding, *There Is a River*, 8–9.
24. Stamp, *The Peculiar Institution*, 144.
25. Mbiti, *Introduction to African Religion*, 102.

obligation of togetherness. The shared space of one African to another is religious in nature; for instance, "since African Religion belongs to the people, no individual member of the society concerned can stand apart and reject the whole of his people's religion."[26] This mentality is seen in the Ashanti lived experience. For the Ashanti, "*the family* is not a small, single unit. It is a unified group, to be sure, but the total group consists of a number of integrated parts, each of which functions in its own sphere."[27] Moreover, "In the Ashanti Kingdom of West Africa, one observer noted that 'a slave might marry; own property; himself become heir to his master. An Ashanti slave, [in] nine cases out of ten, possibly became an adopted member of the family, and in time his descendants so merged and intermarried with the owner's kinsmen that only a few know their origin.'"[28] Similarly, the Nyakyusa religious kinship is so strong that one family member suffering from sin may also cause another family member to suffer. What affects one also affects others.[29]

African religions are founded and passed on through oral traditions. The survival and progression of some faith traditions is contingent upon Africans intermarrying. This creates a broad communal and inter-cultural construct from which one is able to reflect on God, self, and others in an uninhibited and broad manner. Considering the absence of recorded religious reflection from the annals of African history, one can confidently speak of the importance of individual communication within such kinship circles. What is the outcome, however, when such a sociological kinship is traumatically disrupted? What happens to the religious oral traditions that were once passed down from one generation to the next?

The African Religious Experience

Within some social science fields, it is often posited that behavior is best analyzed through the lens of cognitive processes; in other words, a particular belief produces a particular mode of action. If behavior is to be correctly understood, personal beliefs must be fully grasped and appreciated. In a similar manner, religious beliefs produce a particular mode of social behavior. How one thinks about God, death, spirits, self, others, magic, heaven,

26. Ibid., 14.
27. Lystad, *The Ashanti*, 45.
28. Zinn, *A People's History*, 27.
29. Wilson, *Rituals of Kinship*, 233.

Existential Togetherness

and so on[30] factor into how one determines meaning within a particular cultural and geographical location.

At the core of pre-modern thought was the notion that the African religious experience was both uncivilized and lacking definitive methods of approaching the Divine.[31] Such a presupposition is clearly absurd when one considers the intricate nature and structure of African Religion(s). For example, according to mid-sixteenth century slave narratives, adherents of the traditional Ibo religion believed in a Supreme Being. Not only were Africans capable of fostering developed means of engaging religious thought, they were instructed on how to follow such an engagement via a religious leader (e.g., priest). Reflecting on his own African heritage, Olaudah Equiano describes the priesthood as being the embodiment of priests, magicians, and wise men. He states,

> I do not remember whether they had different offices, or whether they were united in the same persons, but they were held in great reverence by the people. They calculated our time, foretold events as their name imported, for we called them Ah-affoeway-cah, which signifies calculators or yearly men. These magicians were also our doctors or physicians.[32]

If this is the case, then why did colonialists reject African genius, indeed their very humanity? Basil Davidson suggests they did so based solely on personal agenda and bias. He contends that "their prejudice and personal feelings made them write that Africans had no history of their own. It is part of the modern rebirth of Africa that we know this view to be entirely untrue.[33]" Africans understood the world as a place of meaning because they could sense God operating in the loftiest as well as in the lowest spaces of life. African peoples possessed an intricate framework from which spirituality was obtained; they viewed God as being foundational to human experience.[34]

African peoples view God within an anthropomorphic frame of reference.[35] Because Africans consider themselves to be at the center of the

---

30. Mbiti, *Introduction to African Religion*, 10.
31. Paris, *The Spirituality of African Peoples*, 23.
32. Ibid, 41.
33. Davidson, *The Growth of African Civilisation*, 1.
34. Ibid., 27–159.
35. Mbiti, *African Religions and Philosophy*, 48.

universe,[36] and because God created, structured, and sustains the universe, one may reasonably gather why African peoples attribute human features to the Supreme Being. This is not to suggest that African peoples equate their being with that of the Supreme Being, but to note that African peoples believe that God possesses human features as a way to engage notions of relational intimacy. God's human characteristics afford Africans the privilege of viewing God as an intimate power with tangible and accessible qualities. Referring to God as Father provides a sense of well-being and protection for African peoples.

> Many visualize God as Father, both in terms of His position as the universal Creator and Provider, and in the sense of his personal availability to them in the time of need. The Akamba consider the heavens and the earth to be the Father's 'equal-sized bowls': they are His property both by creation and the rights of ownership; and they contain his belongings. The Lunda, Bemba and others in the same region, speak of God as 'the universal Father' and mankind as His children. The Suk and Baganda hold that God is the Father not only to men but also to the divinities and other spiritual beings. The idea of God being the Father of creation in general is reported among other peoples, some of whose only or major personal name for God simply means 'father.'[37]

There is a common belief that both indigenous Africans and those located in the diaspora believe that God is transcendent.[38] The reality is a bit more nuanced than that. Indigenous Africans believed that God has the divine power to be intimately involved in the functions of every human reality and yet remain in a Supreme state of transcendence. Unlike a westernized view of God, whereby God's transcendence is separated based upon human interpretations of what is deemed sacred or profane, indigenous Africans believed that all human activity derives from God. Therefore, they identify human activities in and of themselves as being sacred. Moving from Africa to America, newly enslaved Africans consequently were torn between keeping their centuries-old beliefs and re-defining meaning within the context of the unfamiliar cosmology of the Christian West.

Because African religion is transferred both orally and generationally through a specific people and land, African religion is dynamic only as it

---

36. Ibid.
37. Ibid., 68.
38. Ibid., 22.

remains in African society. The only way African religion can exist outside its original geographic location is when Africans carry the message with them to another space and location.[39] We see the former in the narrative of an ex-slave known as Sister Kelly.[40] She dictated a religious experience in which she participated in a clandestine worship service among the enslaved, mentioning using an old pot to muffle the sounds of the worship. Such an experience is reminiscent of what could have occurred with "traditional West African sacrificial vessels."[41]

Raboteau posits that Africans gradually lost certain cosmological content to their religious beliefs and practices as a result of enduring the process of being enslaved.[42] Although enslaved Africans lost their religion's "sacred symbols, ritual practices, particular divinities and ancestral spirits,"[43] the essence of African religion remained the same in that they continued to believe in a transcendent God—this time of the diaspora—who was also responsible and maintained watchful care over the lives of the enslaved Africans.

Community and Personhood

African community is comprised of a unit or group of individuals who share a common interest. It was this deep sense of community that afforded the newly enslaved African the ability to survive the Middle Passage, and ultimately to endure the entire grotesque experience of the American institution of slavery. African peoples have consistently treasured the familial aspect of their existence, as we see in the South African term *Ubuntu*, which speaks to what it means to be dependent upon human togetherness:

> Religion in African communities is written in its members' hearts, minds, oral history, rituals, priests, rainmakers, elders, and kings. There are no sacred scriptures, only traditions. Every individual carries religious traditions from generation to generation. The individual is part of a community in which religion is primary. There are differences of interpretation respecting myths, rituals, and ceremonies but there is no heresy for there is no orthodoxy.

39. Ibid., 12.
40. See Sister Kelly, "Proud of That 'Ole Time' Religion," 69–75.
41. Ibid., 69–70.
42. Raboteau, *Slave Religion*, 86.
43. Paris, *The Spirituality of African Peoples*, 33.

> The individual can no more detach himself from his religion than he can detach himself from his community, either of which means severance from his roots in the kinship group which is so all pervasive and binding in African ethnic-centered communities. Each individual is a religious being for religion is each individual's whole system of being. Precisely here lies the reason why being African and religious is nearly indistinguishable. Africans journeyed here in chains from highly differentiated and complex cultures. The economic, political, and social organization served the basic ethnic units which were as strong as they were central to African life. Religion was the instrument of cohesion, inextricably interwoven amidst daily concerns and less tangible values.[44]

For African peoples, community meant a strong emphasis on collective responsibility. Moreover, "all agree that the community is a sacred phenomenon created by the supreme God, protected by the divinities, and governed by the ancestral spirits."[45] Every member of the community operates as an intricate part of the overall ethos or reality of the group—the commonly held belief that upon death, family ancestors are available to guide and overlook the fortune of the unit. Even in death, the African is unable to escape the responsibility of the group. According to Peter Paris:

> Families are expected to be grateful for the protection of their ancestors and to reciprocate by performing certain rituals in order to maintain harmonious relations between them. Those rituals include the provision of a splendid funeral (a celebratory homecoming event that ushers the person safely and honorably into the ancestral mode), followed by periodic public memorials usually beginning sometime within the first year (often called "the second funeral"), and, depending on the family's economic situation, subsequent memorial celebrations as often thereafter as possible. The ancestral relationship continues for as long as there are persons alive who knew the person in the flesh. When historical memory ends, and no one can remember them by name, they may be said to have fully died.[46]

Community and personhood were thus interrelated realities for the African. But how does one process the experience of a reality—such as slavery—which seems to be diametrically opposite to that which undergirds a sense of meaning and purpose? Despite the tribal conflicts that were

---

44. Washington, *Black Sects and Cults*, 25–26.
45. Paris, *The Spirituality of African Peoples*, 51.
46. Ibid., 53.

experienced on the African continent by warring peoples, the experience of the captured African under European control was quite different from the experience of being enslaved in Africa. If an African was captured in battle, such an experience would be emphasized by the cultural integration of such a one into the extended family. Freedom was certainly a viable reality; but in the event that freedom was too distant a reality to grasp, at least the enslaved person was certain that he or she would be treated with human dignity.

However, being captured and enslaved by Europeans was a different matter altogether. Once captured, re-constructing tribal affiliation and establishing a bond with others was of the utmost priority. But as many languages were spoken, it would have been difficult to hear and respond to the many pleas and demands echoing from the belly of the slave ships. Before that, and not knowing the process by which enslavement would proceed, perhaps slaves reasoned that they had a chance to return to their kindred so long as they were connected to the land of their cultural experience. The moment the enslavers began the process of takings Africans out of their geographical context—whether to await transport overseas, in ships, or in their destination countries—existential togetherness was born, and the need to put aside tribal disagreements for the much higher goal of survival became the priority of the newly enslaved African. Sterling Stuckey is correct in positing that the "slave ships were the first real incubators of slave unity across cultural lines, cruelly revealing irreducible links from one ethic group to the other."[47] These vessels served two purposes: First, Europeans used ships to traverse the Atlantic in hopes of triangulating the buying, selling, and trading of goods (slaves included). It is probable that tribes that once engaged in warfare with one another, and killed one another, found themselves shackled together in a dark and crowded ship storage area. Because Europeans filled these to the maximum to make the highest possible profit, Africans were packed into ships in such a way that individual movement became utterly impossible. Many died due to this crowded and unsanitary method of transportation. Those who survived this evil trek soon discovered that it was just the beginning of their nightmare. Second, captured Africans understood the value of community. They understood that their survival, let alone freedom, was likely contingent upon forming a sense of togetherness or community. Togetherness entailed them setting aside tribal differences. They had to learn to work together as

47. Stuckey, *Slave Culture*, 1.

Existential Togetherness

a unit, and communicate with purpose for such unification. In this regard, their existence depended upon how effectively they were willing to shift from perpetuating tribal factions to becoming one tribe of many collective voices.

Du Bois posited that aspects of this togetherness for the enslaved suffered as a result of the European slave system, which devalued the individual and castigated those who desired to maintain ideals of strength, courage, and fortitude. Nevertheless, the sense of African togetherness and of leadership that was centered in notions of community, togetherness, and meaning seems to be what helped these enslaved Africans to survive. Although some Africans lost the connection of their religious experiences of Africa, the African priest; although enslaved, remained largely committed to the operating function of his religious office.[48] One priestly requirement

---

48. In his 1903 essay, *Of Faith of our Fathers*, Du Bois posited that African cultural influence diminished during a period in which the African slave trade was at its zenith (i.e., 1750). Stuckey argues: "This leads [Du Bois] to conclude that African influence, by 1750, failed to sustain a belief in African divinity, which made Africans ripe for the religion of resignation and patience Christianity would foster. Had the slave trade not increased dramatically in the last half of the eighteenth century, the argument might be more understandable" (*Slave Culture*, 290–91). Stuckey's rationale centers on the notion that the constant influx of African slaves, devoid of western culture and assimilation, likely spoke of experiences that evoked the African religious tradition that had been so familiar to many enslaved Africans. Additionally, Sobel argues that "It would appear that from the outset of slavery until its end there were, at times, Africans speaking African tongues in America" (*Trabelin' On*, 35). Perhaps Du Bois here overextends the duration of trauma experienced by the African enslaved; additionally, with the acquisition of the English language, the newly imported slaves could very well have been considered *outcasts* among the assimilating slaves. African religion most certainly entailed a belief that the Supreme Being was able to traverse the Atlantic Ocean, deliver, and restore the enslaved to their rightful geographical location. However, belief in lower gods (i.e., ancestors) limited the religious experience of the African, as belief in the lower gods was just as important as worship of the Supreme Being. With the latter being disconnected from the responsibility of familial observation, Du Bois' enslaved African had much to consider regarding existential meaning and purpose.

Having studied under the tutelage of William James at Harvard College, Du Bois likely considered the breakdown of African values to be a direct result of the psychological stress several generations of slaves experienced. The learned behavior associated with being viewed as property disrupted notions of community—slave culture had transitioned the enslaved into a reality of survival of the fittest. James posits that "a chain is no stronger than its weakest link, and life is after all a chain" (James, *The Varieties of Religious Experience*, 136). According to Du Bois, the American institution of slavery had weakened the cohesive structure of the African ideal of community; therefore, by 1750, over three hundred years had been devoted to creating such a persona within the enslaved African psyche. In essence, over three hundred years of searching for meaning via the enslaved

was to remain detached from the worldly[49] experience of chattel slavery. This is not to suggest that the enslaved priest did not feel frustration, anger, and desperation at the unrelenting oppression of the whip and all that it symbolized. But perhaps it made him realize the pivotal nature of his role, that he was "an important figure on the plantation and found his function as the interpreter of the supernatural, the comforter of the sorrowing, and as the one who expressed, rudely but picturesquely, the longing and disappointment and resentment of a stolen people."[50] In a sense, by the signing of the *Emancipation* in 1863, the black preacher had become heavily influenced by notions of African priestly traditionalism, Christian doctrine, and personal convictions regarding how God addressed the social issue of enslavement. When both enslaved and free blacks grappled with their plight in America, the preacher was the individual designated to answer adherents' questions.

The American institution of slavery was a horrific experience for the African community. The systematic approach to the dehumanization of the enslaved African virtually ensured that even vestiges of familial rituals and practice would not survive. However, the enslaved Africans' cosmological understanding of togetherness, coupled with a new Christian religious text to further amplify notions of anthropomorphism, was able to create a religious space whereby community was re-defined, and the expertise of oral tradition introduced many enslaved Africans to the appropriation of a Christian way or perceiving the world. In a sense, the former initiated the process of being both African and American. Rather than live in one cultural reality, enslaved Africans learned to live dialectically as African American slaves.

The combination of priest, community, oral tradition, and Christian religion constructed an African theology that produced a new form of communal and ancestral veneration—slave spirituals. The spirituals are significant because they articulate the experience of being both human and

---

experience positioned enslaved Africans to consider another religious alternative. Du Bois notes, "I had received at Harvard excellent preparation for understanding Freud under the tutelage of William James, Josiah Royce, and George Santayana. At this time psychological measurements were beginning at Harvard with Munsterberg; but the work of Freud and his companions and their epoch-making contribution to science was not generally known when I was writing this book, and consequently I did not realize the psychological reasons behind the trends of human action which the African slave trade involved" ("The Suppression of the African Slave-Trade," 1315).

49. Du Bois, *The Souls of Black Folk*, 137.
50. Du Bois, *The Negro*, 113.

slave.[51] "Even a casual examination of those lyrics," argues Paris, "reveals the image of the family permeating the slave's worldview. References to father, mother, brothers, sisters, uncles, aunts, as well as of the extended family of preachers, deacons, and fellow-sinners are commonplace throughout the spirituals."[52] For the newly enslaved African, the duality of being both human and slave was seen in the African cultural expression of song.

> Slavery chain done broke at last, broke
> at last, broke at last
> Slavery chain done broke at last,
> Going to praise God till I die.
>
> Way down in-a dat valley,
> Praying on my knees;
> Told God about my troubles,
> And to help me ef-a He please.
>
> I did tell him how I suffer,
> In de dungeon and de chain,
> And de days I went with head bowed down,
> And my broken flesh and pain.
>
> I did know my Jesus heard me,
> 'Cause de spirit spoke to me,
> And said, "Rise my child, your chillum,
> And you shall be free.
>
> "I done 'p'int one mighty captain
> For to Marshall all my hosts,
> And bring my bleeding ones to me,
> And not one shall be lost."
>
> Slavery chain done broke at last, broke
> at last, broke at last,
> Slavery chain done broke at last,
> Going to praise God till I die.[53]

51. Levine, *Black Culture and Black Consciousness*, 33.
52. Paris, *The Spirituality of African Peoples*, 57.
53. Cone, *The Spirituals and Blues*, 41–42.

Existential Togetherness

At times, the words to slave spirituals can seem to be burdensome; however, "For all their inevitable sadness, slave songs were characterized more by a feeling of confidence than of despair."[54] This confidence was geared toward re-developing meaning in a geographical location that negated the very essence of African existence; through song, slaves were able to articulate a plethora of human emotion without the hermeneutical gaze of the white slave owner. These songs of joy and frustration provided glue to a fractured community. Although the experience of enslavement damaged African notions of togetherness, spirituals afforded slaves the opportunity to come together and construct narratives that provided a context of meaning and purpose despite slavery. Therefore, singing was by nature communal.

Through being disconnected from the names of African ancestors, the African enslaved persons appropriated their new familial worldview as a way of continuing to hold to the sacred notion of honoring one's ancestors. According to Paris:

> Thus, the inclusion of Moses, Joshua, Daniel, Mary, Jonah, or Paul in their spirituals was tantamount to granting them membership in the African realm of the spirit. Further, all slaves expected reunion with their families in heaven, and to that end they often sent messages to them through the spirits of the dying and gave careful attention to the care of the graves. In many and varied ways, their belief in ancestral spirits was kept alive, and most believed that their souls would return to Africa after death, where they would be reunited with their ancestors.[55]

Rather than disavow a cosmological worldview of community, the African enslaved sought to maintain a sense of meaning and purpose by re-constructing how the community was experienced under the oppressive system of slave-holding Christianity. Whether it was the living honoring the deceased ancestor, or the deceased returning to maintain watch over and care for the surviving community, the primary purpose for such an engagement was to remain together. Living Africans gathered meaning and purpose for their lives by believing that a significant part of their existence was with them in spirit although physically absent. The deceased African ancestors gathered meaning according to the long established cosmological beliefs of African community by maintaining a connection as observers.

54. Ibid., 40.
55. Ibid., 57.

Existential Togetherness

To understand African community, one must understand that kinship is a critical tenet of the larger African communal construct. "[I]n fact, some contend that kinship constitutes the whole of Africa tribal community, since all the people are believed to be descended from a common ancestor who long ago lived in their territory, married, produced children, and lives now in the spirit world,"[56] writes Cone, and he continues, "The African family is therefore the natural extension of blood lines held together by the ordinary functions of family life, in which each member shares responsibilities and obligations. The communal nature of the African family affects all relationships within that sphere."[57] Outside of their geographic origin, Africans are transient in terms of how the collective body, acting as one, continues to interpret reality through oral dissemination; so much so, "Africans take great care in teaching their genealogies to their children in order to instill in them a profound sense of familial belonging and a deep pride in their heritage, both of which aid in inculcating in them the sacred obligation to extend the family line."[58] Relational hierarchy is another tenet of the African community. Whenever two persons meet, seniority is quickly ascertained to establish who should take the leadership role.[59] This became an important aspect of enslaved society.

African togetherness was problematic for the enslavers since Africans found strength and community in numbers. The newly enslaved African was "found easier to deal with if they were separated from their kinsmen."[60] Moreover, African social organization of unity and togetherness was sometimes displayed in ways in which certain slaves were designated as the leader for certain slave groups. Such leaders fought to maintain a sense of African remembrance within the newly engaged social dynamic of the institution of slavery. Unfortunately, some slaves were met with the opposition from *accustomed slaves* who had disavowed any connection to any religious familial heritage. In 1859, four native Africans were met with visceral and contempt by acculturated slaves.

> Our common darkies treat them with sovereign contempt walking around them with a decided aristocratic air. But the Africans are docile and very industrious and are represented as being perfectly

---

56. Ibid., 77.
57. Ibid., 79.
58. Ibid., 83–84.
59. Ibid., 86.
60. Frazier, *The Negro Family*, 6.

delighted with their new homes and improved conditions. The story that they are brutes and savages is all stuff and nonsense. It was put in the papers by men who do not know what they are talking about. As to their corrupting our common [N]egroes, we venture to ascertain we would come near[er] the truth if stated the other way.[61]

The only inheritance the majority of newly acculturated slaves understood was presented in a new identity of meaninglessness, subordination, and isolation. They were stolen from their religious and cultural contexts of meaning and worth. Slavers disrupted their African communal identity by intentionally separating slaves as a means of deconstructing familial and tribal communication.

However, we have seen that there were forms of existential togetherness among Africans prior to them being introduced to the overwhelming experience of western civilization. For instance, the Amistad mutiny is a historical narrative about newly enslaved Africans working together as a means of securing freedom; and although language barriers initially prevented investigators from hearing the Africans' story, a Yale professor learned the rudiments of their tongue and began repeating numbers that he had learned from strangers on the street. Fortunately, one native African understood the language to be his own. His interpretations aided in a favorable Supreme Court decision.[62]

Existential togetherness has certainly been a perennial theme in African religious heritage. It is also basis of kinship, and honors the commitment to God, self, and others. Even within the experience of death, the African common religious heritage founded in community attempts to maintain some form of togetherness by engaging in familiar funeral rituals. Whether in life or in death, the African is always connected to the cultural notion of existential togetherness.

There is meaning in functioning as a cohesive unit. Each individual works well as a single unit, knowing that the individual contribution determines the stability of the group, and so each individual is highly valued as an indispensable part of the group. Enslavement, torture, and trauma tested this strong ancestral bond of existential togetherness. The introduction between Africans and Europeans was essentially combative from the very beginning. The enslaved fought to obtain freedom while the enslaver

---

61. Ibid., 7–8.
62. Mullane, *Crossing the Danger Water*, 100–105.

fought to negate African freedom and existence. Religion would become the primary source to support both positions, and it commenced when Europeans set foot in North America. They did not travel alone; along with the idea of expansion, they also brought disease, death, religious ideology, and notions of further geographical expansion and domination.[63]

Christianity and Modernity

The existential question of meaning and purpose has prompted many a human to explore, build, and expand. Since its inception, individuals have used Christianity as a means to substantiate their own avarice by insisting on their divine privilege. The cultural effect of such a movement invariably causes conflict as geographical expansion affords space for one group but marginalizes another. The use of religion, with its emphasis on divine favor, has grounded the rationale behind *nulli secundus* conquests. Frantz Fanon aptly states, "The colonialist bourgeoisie is aided and abetted in the pacification of the colonized by the inescapable powers of religion."[64] With the aid of the Christian religion, men transformed the known world into their notion of centeredness.

> For if anyone has written or said anything about these islands, it was all with obscurities and conjectures; no one claims that he had seen them; from which they seemed like fables. Therefore let the king of other countries of Christendom give thanks to our Lord Saviour Jesus Christ, who has bestowed upon us so great a victory and gift. Let religious processions be solemnized; let sacred festivals be given; on earth, as he rejoices in heaven, when he foresees coming to salvation so many souls of people hitherto lost. Let us be glad also, as well on account of the exaltation of our faith, as on account of the increase of our temporal affairs, of which not only Spain, but universal Christendom will be partaker. These things that have been done are thus briefly related. Farewell.[65]

Peoples of the world construct what is considered sacred based on notions of phenomenological manifestations (i.e., hierophanies).[66] Such manifestations are subsequently interpreted through a framework of

---

63. Blassingame, *The Slave Community*, 4–5.
64. Fanon, *The Wretched of the Earth*, 28.
65. Columbus, "Christopher Columbus Reports His First Impressions of America."
66. Eliade, *The Sacred and the Profane*, 11.

peoples' profane worlds. Within the context of Christianity, Jesus being God incarnate is a sacred symbol for those interpreting such an experience through worldly (i.e., profane) perspectives. As a means of identification and signification, Christians use the cross as a symbol of understanding the nature of their sacred and profane experience.[67] Thus, the positioning of the Christian cross at a particular location communicates the approval of God regarding the human choice of said existential location.

> Here, then, we have a sequence of religious conceptions and cosmological images that are inseparably connected and form a system that may be called the "system of the world" prevalent in traditional societies: (a) a sacred place constitutes a break in homogeneity of space; (b) this break is symbolized by an opening by which passage from one cosmic region to another is made possible (from heaven to earth and vice versa; from earth to the underworld); (c) communication with heaven is expressed by one or another of certain images, all of which refer to the axis mundi: pillar, ladder (cf. Jacob's ladder), mountain, tree, vine, etc.; (d) around this cosmic axis lies the world (our world), hence the axis is located "in the middle," at the "navel of the earth"; it is the center of the world.[68]

The *axis mundi* (e.g. the Christian cross) is a cosmological indication of a balance in which the sacred intersects with the profane to create a sense of centeredness. To be sure, the notion of centeredness is subjective in nature. For instance, if a particular people, deity, and/or space entails a relational reality that defines religion as being centered, it is equally possible to argue that a particular location in which this symbiosis occurs (such as a sanctuary in the Temple in Jerusalem) is geo-religiously centered.[69]

The sacred introduced or identified in a particular profane space is considered the foundation of existence,[70] and gives existential meaning to an otherwise meaningless and futile existence. This particular location then promotes as a means of creating an expansion of meaning regarding scared purpose and the foundational ordering of a social structure (i.e., society).

> The social world intends, as far as possible, to be taken for granted. Socialization achieves success to the degree that this

67. Ibid., 11.
68. Ibid., 37.
69. Ibid., 43.
70. Ibid., 63.

taken-for-granted quality is internalized. It is not enough that the individual look upon the key meanings of the social order as useful, desirable, or right. It is much better if he looks upon them as inevitable, as part and parcel of the universal "nature of things." If that can be achieved, the individual who strays seriously from the socially defined programs can be considered not only a fool or a knave, but a madman. Subjectively, then, serious deviance provokes not only moral guilt but the terror of madness . . . In other words, institutional programs are endowed with an ontological status to the point where to deny them is to deny being itself—the being of the universal order of things and, consequently, one's own being in this order.[71]

As the *nomos* of a society[72] objectively informs the legitimation of social institutions, the people in a given society begin to establish personal credos that substantiate the overall legitimation of a particular social norm. What is deemed to be culturally taboo in one social context may be considered normative in another. The degree to which a taboo is legitimatized depends on the generational indoctrination of a social belief; additionally, such a legitimation must be reiterated to maintain and perpetuate a particular social pattern from one generation to the next.[73]

> Any exercise of social control also demands legitimation over and above the self-legitimating facticity of the institutional arrangements—precisely because this facticity is put in question by the resisters who are to be controlled. The sharper such resistance, and the sharper the means employed to overcome it, the more important will it be to have additional legitimations. Such legitimations serve both to explain why the resistance cannot be tolerated and to justify the means by which it is also quelled. One may say, then, that the facticity of the social world or of any part of it suffices for self-legitimation as long as there is no challenge.[74]

Christian religionists legitimated societal processes for the sole purpose of establishing a nexus between God and human governance. Charles Long is correct in stating that "from that time until the twentieth century, the Western world, through conquest, trade, and colonialism, made contact with every part of the globe. These encounters and confrontations with

---

71. Berger, *The Sacred Canopy*, 24.
72. Ibid., 30.
73. Ibid., 30–31.
74. Ibid., 31.

other cultures raised again the issue of religion."[75] Eventually, the dominant religion of Christians used physical control and intimidation to expand in ideology, wealth, and position. Situated between God's providence and human religious zeal, Christianity became a driving force behind the establishment of a religious milieu that established and perpetuated the racial designation of black being opaque, other, and antithetical to the purpose of God's divine intention.

In the second century, the Christian religion was an organic fellowship belonging to a single and undivided communion united in Christ. The sign of this unity was seen in the personhood of bishop. As Ignatius puts it in one of his letters, "wherever the bishop is, there one finds the fellowship; just as wherever Jesus Christ is there is the Catholic Church.'"[76] Several centuries later, Ignatius' words would prove prophetic. In 1441 "just half a century before Christopher Columbus crossed the Atlantic, there sailed from Portugal to Africa 'a little ship' under the command of one Antam Goncalvez."[77] To win admiration from Prince Henry, Goncalvez sought to capture indigenous people off the coast of Africa.[78] He and nine others waited until the perfect opportunity presented itself.

> Should they persist or go back? Heat, fatigue and thirst discouraged the raiders. They decided to give up. But while returning over the sand-warm dunes to the sea, 'they saw a naked man following a camel, with two assegais in his hand, and as the other men pursued him there was not one who felt aught of his great fatigue. But though he was only one, and saw the others that they were many, yet (this African) had a mind to prove those arms of his right worthily and began to defend himself as best he could, shewing a bolder front than his strength warranted. But Affonso Goterres wounded him with a javelin, and this put the moor in such fear that he threw down his arms like a beaten man. The Portuguese took him prisoner and then, 'as they were going on their way, they saw a Black Mooress come along' and they seized her too.[79]

When the captured Africans were taken to see Prince Henry, the prince was convinced that further raids and conquest would prove most

---

75. Long, *Significations*, 3.
76. Wilken, *The First Thousand Years*, 30.
77. Davidson, *The African Slave Trade*, 53.
78. Ibid.
79. Ibid., 54.

beneficial to him; however, he needed the Church (i.e., the Pope) to grant "to all of those who shall be engaged in said war, complete forgiveness of sin."[80]

The onus of societal control invariably derived from the powerful religious and political influence of the Church. The Church also established doctrinal patterns that aided the indoctrination of legitimation. Although contention was certainly a reality for the early Church's legitimation (e.g., doctrinal conflict among the Gnostics, Marcionites, and Montanists), sacred space and symbolic expression provided enough legitimation to reinforce not only an isolated eastern cultural belief, but also to expand its idealism to Western Europe[81]—to such a degree that Christian themes are even displayed in fifteenth-century cultural artifacts such as art.[82]

Likewise, from the very moment the Spanish conquerors stepped onto the soil of the New World, they observed solely for the purpose of subjugation; "these Spanish soldiers and adventurers, ruined the American peoples whom they found. Their intention was not trade, but loot; not peace, but war; not partnership, but enslavement. They did not travel alone; along with the idea of expansion, they also brought disease, death, and religious ideology."[83] They fell upon these lands with greed and the fury of destruction. And the American peoples, unlike the Africans, were unable to defend themselves.[84]

Columbus, Cortes, Culture, and Conquest

Cristobal Colón (i.e., Christopher Columbus)[85] looked upon the naked bodies of the natives of this *New World* with European contempt and superiority. He saw a people without cultural sophistication, religion, and existential meaning.[86] He stepped into a cultural experience unlike his own and perceived the natives to be uncouth. Because they were unapologetically naked bodies, and because Columbus was an advocate for European

---

80. Ibid., 55.
81. Latourette, *A History of Christianity*, 275–371.
82. Ibid., 654; also see Malraux, *The Voices of Silence*, 436–51.
83. Blassingame, *The Slave Community*, 4–5.
84. Davidson, *The Growth of African Civilisation*, 195.
85. Ibid., 26.
86. Ibid., 35.

decorum, the natives perceived lack of cultural awareness implied a certain inferiority, which awakened in the newcomers notions of conquest.

> They [natives] . . . brought us parrots and balls of cotton and spears and many other things, which they exchanged for the glass beads and hawks' bells. They willingly traded everything they owned . . . They were well-built, with good bodies and handsome features… They do not bear arms, and do not know them, for I showed them a sword, they took it by the edge and cut themselves out of ignorance. They have no iron. Their spears are made of cane…They would make fine servants . . . With fifty men we could subjugate them all and make them do whatever we want.[87]

How did Columbus come to be there? Ferdinand of Aragon and Isabella of Castile were attempting to establish Spain as a world power by means of Christian propagation and geographical expansion.[88] Upon successful negotiation of exploration details, Columbus set out to locate Japan and verify Marco Polo's lofty assertions regarding Asiatic potentiality. Inadvertently, however, he had mistaken Mexico as Japan.[89] In 1493, Columbus returned to Spain to boast of his success; and desiring to further its global position of power, Ferdinand and Isabella sanctioned Columbus' continued explorations in the name of king, queen, and God. Whereas "before that time Spain had always been a poor country. For a century, however, through its monopoly of the gold and silver of America, it dominated the world."[90]

Due to the lack of cultural commonality between Columbus and the natives, the Americas were now subject to whomever the Spaniards thought God deemed physically strong enough to control the land. Although notions of religious commitment, rather than mere interest in obtaining wealth, motivated Columbus' ambitious trek into the unknown,[91] his interpretation of the Christian religion demanded that monies be allocated under the guise of furthering God's desire for European expansion. He was motivated by obtaining wealth as it was his intention to collect enough gold to finance Spain's conquest of Jerusalem.[92]

87. Zinn, *A People's History*, 1.
88. Wells, *The Outline of History*, 618.
89. Ibid.
90. Ibid., 624.
91. Todorov, *The Conquest of America*, 9.
92. Ibid., 12.

Coupled with Hernando Cortes' defeat of the Aztecs, the idea of the *other* was absolutely defined as peoples lacking the racial ingenuity of Europeans.[93] This *othering* was profoundly evident in the expansion of North America via the American institution of slavery. Philosophically understanding the then regnant Christian concept of human personality is beneficial here. Human personality is approved and appreciated by the divine; therefore, humanity should observe a bit of God in every portion of humanity. Defining the *other* based on cultural variances is ridiculous and theologically illogical. Yet such purportedly *Christian* irrationality drove Columbus. It informed his vision of manifest destiny, and substantiated his notions that non-Europeans were the *other*.[94]

Purveyors of such Christian thought produced the greatest atrocity in United States history, perhaps even in human history. White religious leaders argued that slavery was the will of God.[95] Via Bible, gun, dog, and rope, Europeans established a social means of acculturating liberated people into enslaved human beings. From the perspective of the enslaved African, the Christian religion was used to establish an ideology of cultural shamefulness and subjugation. Religion was the justification for enslavement. Religion was also used to indoctrinate a sense of African meaninglessness. The moment Africans walked upon the shores of the New World, they had to grapple with cruel treatment, a new language, new culture, new existence, and new religion. As a result of European notions of the divine right of such religious conquest and their greed for gold and other kinds of wealth, "by 1800, 10 to 15 million blacks had been transported as slaves to the Americas. It is roughly estimated that Africa lost 50 million human beings to death and slavery in those centuries we call the beginnings of modern Western civilization."[96]

> Modern (European) civilization understands itself as the most developed, the superior, civilization. (2) This sense of superiority

---

93. Ibid., 58.

94. Physically naked, the Indians are also [in Columbus's eyes] deprived of all cultural property: they are characterized, in a sense, by the absence of customs, rites, and religion (which has a certain logic, since for a man like Columbus, human beings wear clothes following their expulsion from Paradise). Here there is also his habit of seeing things as it suits him; but it is significant that it leads him to the image of spiritual nudity: "It seemed to me that all these people were very poor in everything," he writes upon his first encounter, and again: "It has seemed to me that they belonged to no religion" (ibid, 35.)

95. See Harrison, *Gospel among the Slaves*.

96. Zinn, *A People's History*, 29.

obliges it, in the form of a categorical imperative, as it were, to "develop" (civilize, uplift, educate) the more primitive, barbarous, underdeveloped civilizations. (3) The path of such development should be that followed by Europe in its own development out of antiquity and the Middle Ages. (4) Where the barbarian or the primitive opposes the civilizing process, the praxis of modernity must, in the last instance, have recourse to the violence necessary to remove the obstacles to modernization.[97]

Both Columbus and Cortes were privileged Spaniards seeking opportunities to expand said privilege. One means of expansion was in the realm of exploration. Exploration entails a degree of comparison; for instance, Columbus deduced the irrelevance of the Indians based on his interpretation of their lack of sophistication of language, culture, and religion. He considered his subjective position as superior and negated the objective reality of the other. According to Todorov, "it is because both rest on a common basis, which is the failure to recognize the Indians, and the refusal to admit them as a subject having the same rights as oneself, but different."[98]

Although Columbus was an outsider, and acknowledged this reality, he nevertheless refused to consider the reality that was present before his arrival. And if he did consider the inside reality, it was lacking his creative stroke of improvement. Todorov aptly states, "He does not perceive alterity, as we have seen, and he imposes his own values upon it; yet the term by which he most often refers to himself and which his contemporaries also employ is extranjero, *outsider*."[99] His outsiderness differs from that of Cortes in that he negated the lived experience of the other as a valid reality. His animalistic signification of the Indian diminished their human capacity of ingenuity and innovation; although his weapons were much more sophisticated, he failed to consider the cultural importance and worthiness of their contributions. Cortes, on the other hand, wanted to understand the essence of the Native lived experience. "What Cortes wants from the first is not to capture but to comprehend."[100] He is enthralled with comprehending the cultural variations of the explored geography. To be sure, Cortes is still a privileged explorer seeking to expand his privileged state; however, he does it with a more nuanced expression of conquest.

97. Dussell, *Eurocentrism and Modernity*, 75.
98. Todorov, *The Conquest of America*, 49.
99. Ibid., 50.
100. Ibid., 99.

Existential Togetherness

As a result of understanding the cultural signification of the other, Cortes had gained an important advantage; for instance, he is viewed as a liberator, rather than a conqueror. "Cortes often appears to them as a lesser evil, as a liberator, so to speak, who permits them to throw off the yoke of a tyranny especially detestable because so close at hand."[101] The Aztecs had already laid the groundwork for Cortes. They had defined what it meant to be conquered. Mexico had learned through experience what it meant to be marginalized and considered less than. Cortes did not have to fully diminish their human dignity; it had already been done. Any minute progression under the "oppressive" system of Cortes was viewed as a liberative experience. It is difficult for the colonizer to harbor appreciation for the colonized because the colonizer operates simply as a dominant subjective being—unable to appreciate the otherness associated with the experience of the colonized.

Modernity commenced in 1492.[102] "From the time of the voyages of Columbus through the nineteenth century, European hegemony was established through economic, technological, military, and, to a certain extent, religious means throughout the world. This was, in the words of Immanuel Wallerstein, the beginnings of the modern world systems."[103]

> Europeans had declared themselves owners and governors of the lands of others—nonwhite, heathen others. Then, when these others finally and inevitably resisted, Europeans were regularly "forced into a lawful offensive war" against them to "revenge affronts and murders. Since the Europeans had brought the laws of their churches and states with them, they could decimate the others legally and morally, in apparent quietness and righteousness of conscience. The Euro-American search for "peace" by means of legal genocide had begun, and the drive to possess this country was won.[104]

Columbus, representing Southern European notions of expansion, was hired to navigate the oceans and discover both land and opportunity for wealth. It is at this point in history that Europe established a geographical location that served its interests in world domination. This domination was not only geographical; through various means of *othering*, Europe also

---

101. Ibid., 58.
102. Dussel, *Eurocentrism and Modernity*, 65–76.
103. Long, *Significations*, 110.
104. Harding, *There Is a River*, 25.

dominated non—European humans. Thus, coupled with Cortes' defeat of the Aztecs, the idea of the *other* was absolutely defined as peoples lacking the particular racial ingenuity seen in the lives of Europeans.[105] The former idea would become profoundly evident in the expansion of North America via the American institution of slavery.

Christianity was a leading element in Columbus and Cortes' overall ethos.[106] It informed their vision of manifest destiny, and substantiated their notions that non—Europeans were heathens. Furthermore, slavery was argued from a position of religious necessity. Disagreeing with slavery was tantamount to defying the very utterances of the divine.

European Ethical Hypocrisy

John Donne is correct in stating that, "No man is an island, entire of itself; every man is a piece of the continent, a part of the main."[107] Being a theologian and preacher, John Donne presents a type of ecclesiastical recommendation regarding Christian global initiatives. In a sense, he posits that what affects the *other*, most certainly also affects him indirectly. Unfortunately, several of Donne's contemporaries believed that Christian global initiatives entailed the furtherance of white Christianity, slavery, and colonization. They did not consider, however, the psychological and philosophical implications of slavery. Diminishing the personhood of another also indirectly diminishes the personhood of the perpetrator. An authentic human being cannot, in good conscience, enslave the mind, body and soul of another without experiencing the same harsh effects.[108]

In 1776, thirteen English colonies submitted a *Declaration of Independence* to Great Britain. The intersectional engagement of religion and politics assisted American colonists in constructing a document that substantiated the realities and privileges of personhood: "We hold these truths to be self-evident, that all men are created equal, that they are endowed by their Creator with certain unalienable Rights, that among these are Life, Liberty and the pursuit of Happiness."[109] In other words, human beings (principally meaning various political and ecclesial leaders in Great

---

105. Todorov, *The Conquest of America*, 54.
106. Ibid., 9–10.
107. Donne, *Selected Poems*, 143.
108. Salzberger and Turck, *Reparations for Slavery*, 48.
109. Du Bois, *The Negro*, 110.

Britain) were disrupting God-ordained privileges of other human beings. As such, colonists deemed it only fair to resort to bloodshed as a means of living the most authentic existence (i.e., freedom of body and thought). Yet, "there were half a million slaves in the confines of the United States when the *Declaration of Independence*"[110] was drafted.

African Religious Acculturation

Monumental victories over both the Moors and Jews assisted in developing a theological mentality that God was involved in the process of establishing divine order through God's instrument, Spain.[111] Columbus possessed a spirit of triumphalism.[112] This privileged thought of self is seen in Columbus' ability to 1) murder people, 2) take possession of their land, and 3) claim that God ordained such actions. Elsa Tamez argues that all conquering peoples possess a perception of concept before experience.[113] The former is seen in how conquerors possessed a blatant disregard for the *other* having previous ownership and knowledge within any given experience. Such a disregard for the *other* is predicated upon a belief that *otherness* is antithetical to Christian beliefs; therefore, God ordained instruments (e.g., Spain) are mandated to expose the *other* to Christianity via warlike tendencies as outlined in biblical narrative (e.g., the book of Joshua).[114]

---

110. Ibid.
111. Ibid., 14.
112. Ibid.
113. Ibid.
114. The Old Testament narrative of Joshua as destroyer coincides with the premise that conquering peoples seem to appropriate God as the basis for their divinely sanctioned actions. Joshua became a *de facto* conqueror when he chooses to take possession of lands that belonged to other peoples. There is a nautical similarity in the Joshua and Columbus narratives. Columbus, for instance, sails the oceans to new opportunity; likewise, Joshua and the children of Israel cross the River Jordan to gain access to land and opportunity. God, no doubt, has enabled them to have success. "When your children ask their parents in time to come, 'What do these stones mean?' then you shall let your children know, 'Israel crossed over the Jordan here on dry ground.' For the Lord your God dried up the waters of the Jordan for you until you crossed over, as the Lord your God did to the Red Sea, which he dried up for us until we crossed over, so that all peoples of the earth may know that the hand of the Lord is mighty, and so that you may fear the Lord your God forever (Josh 4:21—24).

From the Mayan prophet Chilam Balaam to Pablo Richard,[115] several non-European agents provided both logical and ethical reasons to reject the Christian canon. In a letter to Pope John Paul II,[116] some argued that the Bible was used as a weapon of mass destruction. To be sure, Columbus et al., used the Bible to reject established religious and cultural traditions of the indigenous and replaced them with European ideological preferences.

For many westerners, it is difficult to integrate indigenous traditions into the closed Christian canon. But "Gustavo Gutierrez is correct when he states that if we were Indigenous, we would think in another manner."[117] The Bible and indigenous hermeneutics are found in the African experience of enslavement. Being conquered entailed being culturally deprived of all personal and collective sensibilities.

> During the Middle Passage, mortality from undernourishment and disease was about 16 percent. The first few weeks of the trip was the most traumatic experience for the Africans. A number of them went insane and many became so dependent that they gave up the will to live. Slaves in the latter condition were described as having the "fixed melancholy."[118]

The African religious hermeneutic, however, entailed a commitment that, despite being culturally isolated, inspired the enslaved African to discover meaning and purpose in the most nefarious actions. For many a slave, their introduction into the Christian religion shifted the form and construction of the worship experience. The enslaved African merely integrated Christian religious practices with that of an African hermeneutic.

> Here is a definition of the hermeneutic concept and task as it is explained by Ebeling: The word of God must be left free to assert itself in an unflinchingly critical manner against distortions and fixations. But . . . theology and preaching should be free to make a translation into whatever language is required at the moment and to refuse to be satisfied with correct, archaizing repetition of 'pure doctrine.'[119]

---

115. Tamez, "The Bible and Five Hundred Years of Conquest," 18.
116. Ibid.
117. Ibid., 22.
118. Blassingame, *Slave Community*, 7.
119. Mitchell, *Black Preaching*, 18.

Existential Togetherness

The acculturation process of the enslaved entailed both physical and psychological trauma. The African psyche was certainly influenced by the constant stream of negative notions regarding one's cultural African heritage; coupled with floggings, beatings, rape, and mutilation, it is reasonable to conclude the range of difficulty regarding retaining a positive sense of self.

But the newly enslaved African survived; and with a new cultural frame of reference to consider, slaves searched for familiar cultural remnants in a religious society that they could not understand. They managed to associate American cultural variations with similar cultural expressions as experienced in an African context. Religious understanding has always been at the core of African religion; although re-locating to another land caused a disruption, such an expedition was not enough to totally destroy the religiosity that had been established for thousands of years. The essence of religious community is so entrenched in the African psyche that it is nearly offensive to suggest that anything African has survived. Levine is reluctant to use the term *survival* to describe elements of Africanism. But survive it did.

> Scholars must be receptive to the possibility that for Africans, as for other people, the journey to the New World did not inexorably sever all associations with the Old World; that with Africans, as with Europeans and Asian immigrants, aspects of the traditional cultures and world view they came which may have continued to exist not as mere vestiges but as dynamic, living, creative parts of group life in the United States. To insist that only those elements of slave culture were African which remained largely unchanged from the African past is to misinterpret the nature of culture itself.[120]

The newly enslaved Africans brought strong memories of family, love, sex, success, failure, family, tribe, clan, land and so on to the Americas. At the core of the former lies the collective notion of religious community. Once situated in the New World, Africans began the process of obtaining a better understanding of their new environment.

What did the word of God mean to the enslaved African? How did the enslaved African translate divine meaning and purpose outside the context of religious familiarity? The Christian notion of God did not differ much from the African notions of divine activity, so African slaves subjectively

---

120. Levine, *Black Culture and Black Consciousness*, 4–5.

interpreted Christian dogma and appropriated it within the context of familiar African religious experiences. Enslaved Africans formed a new hermeneutic[121] in that they translated the tenets of the Christian faith into their mode of understanding (i.e., language and culture). This meant that they developed an alertness to God in every enslaved endeavor. Whether they were harvesting fields, cooking, or cleaning, the enslaved situated God within the center of the experience as a means of coping and garnering strength. Additionally, enslaved Africans hermeneutically believed that this appropriated religion should address subjective needs.[122] Although white-slave holding Christianity subjectively interpreted the Bible to mean the justification of enslavement, slaves used biblical narrative to locate instances of liberation. In a sense, Africans used Christianity to reinforce their personal notions regarding what they knew to be divine activity; even when they were dying because of Christian sanctioned oppression and bondage, enslaved Africans nevertheless held true to their understanding of the whole of Africa being united in life and in death. Not even the horrifying deeds of chattel slavery could totally annihilate the African concept of togetherness. Charles Ball, "the late eighteenth-century Maryland slave who later lived among plantation slaves further south," aptly stated "that the Africans among them believed *universally* that after death they shall return to their own country, and rejoin companions and friends," a belief "founded in their religion."[123]

Although enslaved Africans' religious notions of the divine survived the experience of the Middle Passage, the physical, spiritual, and psychological toil of chattel slavery escorted the enslaved into a state of existential meaningless; after enduring such an experience, Africans had to redefine religious experience under social conditions of African American enslavement. Thus, they acted and believed out of the social context in which slave religion was born.

> Acculturation in the United States involved the mutual interaction between two cultures, with Europeans and Africans borrowing from each other. When the African stepped on board a European ship he left all of the artifacts or physical objects of his culture behind him. In Africa, as in most societies, these objects were far

---

121. Ibid., 20.
122. Ibid., 20–21.
123. Gutman, *The Black Family*, 332.

less important than values, ideas, relationships, and behavioral patterns.[124]

For many a year, slaves were taught how to contract into the religious boundaries set by slave masters. They were taught that Christianity was an important component of social stratification. According to racist nomenclature, God ordained that Europeans expand their physical boundaries as a means of fulfilling a destiny of greatness. Such an expansion entitled whites (men in particular) to wealth, land, and free labor. The former social structure was developed and maintained by physical force; but during the intermission of beatings, floggings, rape and murder, religion was used to control and manipulate the enslaved. The genius of the enslaved, however, was the ability to appropriate a positive meaning from a religion that was used to coerce them into brutal submission. Blassingame notes that, "Christian forms were so similar to African religious patterns that it was relatively easy for the early slaves to incorporate them with their traditional practices and beliefs. In America Jehovah replaced the Creator, and Jesus, the Holy Ghost, and the Saints replaced the lesser gods."[125]

Early sociological scholarship posits that enslaved Africans were systematically stripped of their social heritage.[126] This process entailed eradicating any form of cohesion among the slaves; if cultural relevancy remained intact, it exponentially increased the probability of rebellion.[127] Losing one's social heritage also meant losing a significant portion of religious identity, but African religious belief entailed a cultus of ritual that was coded in every facet of their existence.

> Religious beliefs are carried into action through ritual. Closely interwoven with the ritual experience of West African peoples is the vibrant pattern of music. Dancing, drumming, and singing play a constant and integral part in the worship of the gods and ancestors…The gods of Africa were carried in the memories of the enslaved Africans across the Atlantic. To be sure, they underwent a sea change. African liturgical seasons, prescribed rituals, traditional myths, and languages of worship were attenuated, replaced, and altered, or lost. Still, much remained, and particularly in Latin

---

124. Blassingame, *Slave Community*, 20.
125. Ibid., 21.
126. Frazier, *The Negro Church in America*, 9.
127. Gutman, *The Black Family*, 335–36.

America the gods lived on in the beliefs and rituals of the slaves' descendants.[128]

The manner in which Africans dressed, walked, and communicated entailed a participation in religious experience; indeed, the community was part of the ritualistic practice of the African ethos. Therefore, the denial of certain practices and rituals did not totally disavow African religious identity; Africans simply learned to adapt and appropriate religious meaning within the context of a meaningless existence of being enslaved. Thus, slave religion was birthed out of the oppressive introduction to white slave-holding Christianity. As Peter Paris so aptly argues, "Between 1740 and 1780 . . . Vast numbers of African slaves entered into a developing Anglo-American colonial slave society. The slave social class took its formative shape in those decades when so many African men and women encountered the mainstream cultural beliefs and practices of their owners and other whites."[129]

The organic nature of slave religion permeates the religious experience of black people. This includes African notions of the *divine*, which is integrally connected to every component of life. Prior to the European invasion African peoples had a perennial pursuit of religious thought.[130] Moreover, Africans shared the freedom of living in a theological sphere of intense reflection and consideration.

There is a perennial transmission of religious thought within the black psyche.[131] In a sense, it supports what Carl Jung articulates regarding the notion of the collective unconsciousness—that the idea of the divine is a psychological necessity within the thought processes of every individual.[132] There is certainly validity to the claim that some African religious practices were displaced as a result of the diaspora; however, the idea and creativity of the religious experience was never forsaken nor forgotten. It merely shifted in terms of purpose and meaning.

128. Paris, *Virtues and Values*, 15.

129. Gutman, *The Black Family*, 335–36.

130. Raboteau, *Canaan Land*, 9.

131. Melville Herskovits challenged Frazier's position in *The Myth of the Negro Past*. Herskovits and Frazier engaged in *The Great Debate* about African retentions as a means of determining what affect Christianity had on the African American community. Frazier argued that Christianity provided meaning and purpose to a people who's culture was annihilated as a result of slavery; conversely, Herskovits argued that African culture was not annihilated, rather it adopted certain elements of the Christian faith as a means of survival in the Diaspora.

132. See Jung, *The Archetypes and the Collective Unconsciousness*.

Existential Togetherness

Situated in a state of oppressive bondage, the enslaved Africans, however, developed new rituals to address their newly formed relation to the divine. Slaves were not introduced to the reality of God upon arriving in the Americas, but they were introduced to a new religious structure that devalued their worth as human beings. This system was religious in nature. Enslaved Africans were systematically oppressed by religious reminders that their masters were operating at the behest of God. As Kelly Brown Douglas notes, "Others from the slaveholding class did not believe that slavery was a sin. They developed a religious apology for the chattel system—that of slave holding Christianity. The White Christ was the center of this religion. The White Christ characteristically allowed for (1) the justification of slavery, (2) Christians to be slaves, and (3) the compatibility of Christianity with the extreme cruelty of slavery."[133]

As a result of their authentic religious fortitude, slaves observed gaps in how whites preached and practiced tenets of Christianity. Some slaves rejected Christianity as a result of their experience with cruel Christian slave masters. Nevertheless, there were some who could identify with the God of the Bible/Quran, and somehow tailor it to mesh with their personal experience and interpretation of the *divine*.

Slaves would reluctantly hear white clergy preach, but they would actively listen to Black preachers preach and sing. Singing was also a key component in slave religion. The practice lifted spirits and renewed hearts. In hush harbors, slaves were *free* to shout, sing, cry, pray and preach. Raboteau notes that they met

> in secluded places—woods, gullies, ravines, and thickets (aptly called *hush harbors*). Kalvin Woods remembered preaching to other slaves and singing and praying while huddled behind quilts and rags, which had been thoroughly wetted "to keep the sound of their voices from penetrating the air" and then hung up "in the form of a little room," or tabernacle. On one Louisiana plantation, when the "slaves would steal away into the woods at night and hold services," they "would form a circle on their knees around the speaker who would also bow on his knees. He would bend forward and speak into or over a vessel of water to drown the sound. If anyone became animated and cried out, the others would quickly stop the noise by placing their hands over the offender's mouth.[134]

---

133. See Douglas, *The Black Christ*.
134. Raboteau, *Slave Religion*, 215.

Their preaching was less structural modes of oration and more about asking God to connect God's heart to the hearts of the enslaved. Community gatherings were not about gossip. Rather, the purpose of communal gathering was to support one another during the existential realities of continuous pain and suffering. Praying was not a means by which people heard a human voice; just the opposite, it was a means by which the divine interrupted the human voice and settled an oppressed heart. Preaching, praying and singing afforded the enslaved the opportunity to have ownership of religious experiences. The Christian Bible, on the other hand, was used as a means to suppress authentic religious interpretation among the enslaved.

Howard Thurman reminisces about his grandmother and her refusal to read anything related to the apostle Paul, for she had been taught, within the context of Pauline pedagogy, to be obedient to her earthly master. Indeed, "their arguments from the New Testament were based on the apostolic injunctions to obedience and submission on the part of slaves, as implying permission of the relation, and they pointed triumphantly to the Epistle to Philemon as teaching by Paul's example of the duty of apprehending runaways and returning them to their masters."[135]

Such mis-use of Scripture capitalized on the ignorance of the slave. That teaching a slave to read was illegal solidified slave masters' agenda of keeping the true graceful and liberating essence of the *divine* hidden from slaves in order to keep them in their place. Thurman's grandmother was correct in her suspicion regarding this New Testament hermeneutic; as it pertains to the enslaved, the New Testament was the bullet and the slave master had the gun.

Slave holding Christianity may have focused on Pauline literature of the New Testament, but slave religion was committed to the study of Old Testament:

> While slave masters dwelled upon the Pauline doctrine of slave obedience as their entrée' into Christianity, slaves found a different message in the Old Testament. Anointing themselves as the modern counterparts to the Children of Israel, they appropriated the story of Exodus as a parable of their own deliverance from bondage.[136]

The biblical story of Exodus was ripe with metaphoric symbolism for the African enslaved. It provided a context from which they were able to

---

135. Shanks, *The Biblical Anti-Slavery Argument*, 203–16.
136. Berlin, *The Making of African America*, 128.

associate their traumatic experience with that of a similar context. Thus, slaves discovered hope in biblical narrative because they were able to relate to a particular pathos that gave them the strength to cope and the opportunity to develop realistic notions of liberation from their lived experience with an American Pharaoh (i.e., the American institution of chattel slavery).

> African Americans were slaves when they collectively encountered the story of Exodus: it was as slaves that they first learned of this story about slaves. The Bible told of a miraculous mass flight of slaves orchestrated by God himself. At the shore of the *yam suph*, the sea of reeds, the escaping Israelites are pursued by Egyptian chariots and cavalry led by Pharaoh to reclaim the Hebrew fugitives. Pinned between the desert and the sea, the Israelites panic at the sight of Pharaoh's army in the distance. God directs Moses to wave his staff over the sea, which divides and allows the Israelites safe passage. When Pharaoh's army attempts to pursue them, the waters come crashing down on the Egyptians, drowning Pharaoh's entire host. On freedom's shore, the Israelites sing one of the oldest canticles in all of scripture, the song of God's miraculous victory over Pharaoh's chariots.[137]

"The biblical themes most worked upon in popular reading," according to Tamez, "have been the exodus and the historic practice of Jesus, including the cross-resurrection as a paradigmatic axis."[138] The exodus narratives cited above provided an example of a lived experience in which an oppressed people are liberated by God. In *Pillars of Cloud and Fire*, Herbert Marbury describes how African Americans negotiated an Exodus religious hermeneutic via political visions of African American liberation and social transformation in the United States.[139]

Appropriating Exodus as a narrative of relief confirmed for the enslaved that Christianity was mindful of the marginalization and exploitation of God's people. The Exodus narrative gave hope to the struggles of the African enslaved. Further textual critique could also lead one to re-consider if taking ownership of the Exodus narrative is appropriate, considering that the African and Israel slave narratives are only similar in that they both end physical enslavement. The Exodus narrative includes reparations within the overall experience of liberation and freedom of Israel. To be sure, Yahweh understood that economics would provide a perennial existence beyond

---

137. Callahan, *The Talking Book*, 85.
138. Tamez, "The Bible and Five Hundred Years of Conquest," 20.
139. Marbury, *Pillars of Cloud and Fire*, 3–12.

Existential Togetherness

mere physical liberation. Via God's directive, the people were commanded to ask the Egyptians for wealth. "The Israelites had done Moses' bidding and borrowed from the Egyptians objects of silver and gold, and clothing. And the Lord had disposed the Egyptians favorably toward the people, and they let them have their request.[140]" Additionally, the Egyptians were commanded to request certain personal items that held a high economic value. The accumulation of wealth was such that it placed the Egyptians in economic peril. Nevertheless, the Egyptians honored Israel's request, and a liberated people became economically empowered to control their own destiny. The African American slave experience would not yield the same result.

> It must be remembered and never forgotten that the civil war in the South which overthrew Reconstruction was a determined effort to reduce black labor as nearly as possible to a condition of unlimited exploitation and build a new class of capitalists on this foundation. The wage of the Negro worker, despite the war amendments, was to be reduced to the level of bare subsistence by taxation, peonage, caste, and every method of discrimination. This program had to be carried out in open defiance of the clear letter of the law.[141]

The slaves had heard the exodus story preached from both black and white contexts, but the majority of the enslaved could only envision a black liberative hermeneutic. Their traumatized condition did not allow them to grapple intelligently with the different variations associated with being free. Their interpretation did not consider textual structure and historical criticism but of struggle, freedom, and restitution.

Although white slaveholding Christianity did not initiate the pursuit of the *divine* within the slaves' consciousness, it did create a phenomenon in which the black psyche would seek respite from the oppressive systems developed to hinder the expansion of black progression. Slave religion was an experience in which black souls learned to seek relief from daily oppressive forces. For the enslaved, religion became a means of both coping and hoping. Slaves had to endure the barbaric realities of being treated on par with domestic animals, or even worse.

---

140. See Exodus 12: 35–36; Berlin and Brettler, eds., *The Jewish Study Bible*, 120.
141. Du Bois, *Black Reconstruction in America*, 670.

Existential Togetherness

Slavery created a dysfunctional way in which freed blacks experienced God, self, and others.[142] Religious boundaries became blurred when white men decided to expand their religious landscape. Slave religion was the direct result of the U.S.'s religious landscape colliding with the African people's religious landscape; unfortunately, the African physical, social, temporal and territorial boundaries were compromised, and the forced expansion into an unfamiliar context decreased the progressive maturity of a people.

Although African slaves were eventually freed from physical bondage, they lacked the proper resources to expand into a nation that had ambitions of becoming the greatest power in the world. Considering the trajectory of a recovering nation, and its lack of governmental aid for the newly freed black, the early twentieth-century black was on the cusp of existential isolation and meaninglessness.

> The process of enslavement was almost unbelievably painful and bewildering for the Africans. Completely cut off from their native land, they were frightened by the artifacts of the white man's civilization and terrified by his cruelty until they learned that they were only expected to work for him as they had been accustomed to doing in their native land. Still, some were so morose they committed suicide; others refused to learn the customs of whites and held on to the memory of the African cultural determinants of their status.[143]

When slaves found themselves lost in the peculiar institution of American chattel slavery, they oft times discovered a hidden sanctuary in what E. Franklin Frazier identified as the invisible institution.[144] The invisible institution became the antithesis of the peculiar institution of American chattel slavery and the Americanized system of oppression more broadly in years to come. This invisible institution was a phenomenon that created a new paradigm of biblical interpretation. Many elements of African religious practices had not been totally annihilated. What survived was of significant value as enslaved Africans began the process of constructing their own theology and religious foundation as oppressed people (i.e., African Americans).

---

142. See DeGruy, *Post Traumatic Slave Syndrome*.
143. Blassingame, *The Slave Community*, 3–4.
144. Frazier, *The Negro Church in America*, 16; Mitchell, *Black Church Beginnings*, 9.

3

Trauma, Conversion, and the Mythical Meaning of the Slave Preacher

> He early appeared on the plantation and found his function as the healer of the sick, the interpreter of the Unknown, the comforter of the sorrowing, the supernatural avenger of wrong, and the one who rudely but picturesquely expressed the longing, disappointment, and resentment of a stolen and oppressed people. Thus, as bard, physician, judge, and priest, within the narrow limits allowed by the slave system, rose the Negro Preacher, and under him the first Afro-American institution, the Negro Church.[1]

SINCE ITS INCEPTION, THE black church has been a refuge of attention and care. When whites denied blacks the opportunity to engage in various components of society, the black church created a space that provided social justice awareness, educational opportunities, and spiritual meaning for its people. The black preacher has always been at the head of such initiatives. The slave preacher had this type of concern in mind whenever slaves became inspired to worship in the hush/brush harbors; being denied the privilege of authentically worshipping God from an African cosmological frame of reference, slave preachers had to determine when, where, and how to meet in this new context. All of this had to be done in such a way as not to attract attention or suspicion from white masters and overseers. The slave, and then more broadly black preacher, required a certain type of

---

1. Du Bois, *The Souls of Black Folk*, 196.

personality, a personality scholars have discussed and that I present thematically in this chapter.

Characteristics of the Slave Preacher

In the latter part of the nineteenth century, H. T. Kealing describes the black preacher as a great manipulator. He does not, however, treat the black preacher in a negative sense, rather he highlights the preacher's ability "to excite each slumbering emotion of the soul—fear, anger, interest, curiosity, contempt, doubt, hope, anticipation, ecstasy. He plays upon a harp of a thousand strings, its tones varied by almost every appreciable modification of look, gesture, pose, volume, quantity, inflection and pitch."[2] The slave preacher had the ability to relate emotionally and intellectually to the people. He knew the most intimate cares of his fellow-slaves, his congregation. He cared for their individual needs, yet also had to be concerned about how personal behavior affected the group. The black preacher was burdened with the awful task of addressing collective black sorrow. Even in times of difficulty, the black preacher had to advocate for the possibility of a brighter day. Therefore, the slave preacher had to manipulate the emotions of the slave, as a means of inspiring them to focus beyond the events of current pain and suffering. Not that Kealing attaches notions of emotional avoidance to the black parishioner; rather that he suggests the black preacher was astute enough to determine the philosophical underpinnings located within the power of choice. The black preacher knew that a lingering thought of sorrow would become detrimental. Therefore, with rhetorical suasion, the black preacher acknowledged pain and suffering while also reminding the sufferer that *troubles don't last always.*

Much like Kealing's philosophical treatment of the black preacher, Du Bois describes the black preacher as having "the combination of certain adroitness with deep-seated earnestness, of tact with consummate ability."[3] Moreover, as "the centre of a group of men,"[4] Du Bois posits that the black preacher is the most prominent black personality in the country. Early twentieth-century black America, still grappling with the contradictory allusion of emancipation, needed a leader who was intellectually able to lead hordes of marginalized people to a better position in life. For Du Bois, the

2. Kealing, "The Colored Ministers of the South," 140.
3. Du Bois, *Souls of Black Folk*, 190–91.
4. Ibid.

burden of ultimate success for black folk was placed upon the shoulders of the most influential and intellectual person in the black community, the preacher. Dr. Martin Luther King Jr. posited that the slave preacher, as the moral and ethical philosopher of the community, accomplished this by proclaiming a *sense of dignity* and *sense of self-respect* to the slave community. For he recognized that

> every parent must remind his or her child, every minister of the gospel must remind his congregation, every negro must remind his neighbor, his brother, and his sister that we are God's children, and that every man from a bass black to a treble white is significant on God's keyboard [and that] nobody is to make us feel that we are nobody. This is what the old slave preacher used to do. He didn't always have his grammar right. He had never heard of Plato or Aristotle. He would never have understood Einstein's theory of relativity. But he knew God, and he knew that the God that he worshiped was not a God that would subject some of his children and exalt others. And so he looked at his black brothers and sisters and said, "You ain't no niggers. You ain't no slaves. But you're God's children. And this gave them a sense of dignity and a new sense of somebody-ness.[5]

With ingenious audio retention, "Slave preachers often could virtually reproduce the emotional sermons delivered by the white ministers they heard."[6] John Blassingame also illumes the intellect of some slave preachers by stating that they "were remarkably well trained (some of them read Greek, Latin, and Hebrew) or famous for their oratorical skills."[7] Blassingame further notes that the slaves were far from naïve; gifted with unique analytical skills, the slave preacher possessed the ability to construct a new theology from the biased biblical presentations that the masters often used to suppress the liberative spirit of the slaves.

Eugene D. Genovese presents the slave preacher as a troublemaker. Considering the fact that every plantation had a resident preacher, it is rather logical to assume that some slave preachers, as H. Beecher Hicks Jr. concludes, "played a significant role in the social and spiritual development and ultimate destruction of the slave community."[8] Charles Hamilton furthers this thought by suggesting that the black preacher "was expected

---

5. King, *Papers*, 7:477.
6. Ibid.
7. Blassingame, *The Slave Community*, 92.
8. Hicks, *Images of the Black Preacher*, 36.

by the slaveholders to pacify the slaves and reconcile them to their lowly lot here on earth."[9] Raboteau asserts, however, "for some the call to preach might have been a call to status and privilege, but for the majority it was the command of God to spread the Gospel."[10] Thus, the slave preacher was certainly influential within the slave community—for both good and bad purposes. Genovese's treatment, however, must be contextually understood to mean good for slaves, and rather bad for the slave master. There was an instance in Madison County, Alabama in which white preachers were preferred over slave preachers because the latter were "trouble makers."[11] Additionally, "Salomon Oliver was beaten for defying orders not to preach to slaves."[12] Moses Roper, in Blassingame's *Slave Testimony*, recollects on an experience in which a Georgia slave by the name of George was "threatened with 500 lashes from his master if the slave continued to preach to slaves. He continued to preach."[13] To prevent future slave preachers from adopting this trouble maker's mentality, white masters often resorted to cruel and unusual punishment as means to communicate intolerance to violators. For instance, "George was burnt alive within one mile of the court-house at Greenville, in the presence of an immense assemblage of slaves, which had been gathered together to witness the horrid spectacle from a district of twenty miles in extent."[14] Henry Bibb provides an account in which James Smith was converted and desired to preach to fellow slaves, but his master disapproved. To ensure that James did not become what his master perceived to be troublesome, "he was sometimes kept tied all day Sundays while the other slaves were allowed to go just where they pleased on that day. At other times he was flogged until blood would drip down his feet, and yet he would not give up laboring whenever he could get an opportunity, on the Sabbath day, for the conversion of souls."[15]

9. Hamilton, *The Black Preacher in America*, 37.
10. Raboteau, *Slave Religion*, 257.
11. Genovese, *Roll, Jordan, Roll*, 259.
12. Ibid., 246.
13. Blassingame, *Slave Testimony*, 25.
14. Ibid.
15 Ibid., 276–77.

The slave preacher was a privileged individual, according to Albert J. Raboteau,[16] with some allegedly being "exempt from hard manual labor."[17] Slave preachers were also exempt from certain work duties as long as their privilege did not interfere with the work of other slaves.[18] There are instances in which slave preachers refused to accept such privilege as it would detach them from the struggle of the community. The African preacher, Uncle Jack, was offered a new black suit from a "pious and wealthy lady, feeling grieved to see him so rudely clad."[19] He refused such attire as it may have taken his focus away from his call to preach and influence within the community. Thus, there were times in which black privilege could be used for good. Being the foremost leader in the community, the slave preacher often was the first black to receive pertinent information from whites. His job was then to inform the slave community. Raboteau contends "it was from the preacher, this relatively mobile and privileged slave, that the rest first heard of the Civil War."[20]

Some scholarship treats the slave preacher as 1) a great manipulator, 2) an intellectual, 3) a troublemaker, and 4) a privileged individual. A complex individual familiar with personal and collective angst, the slave preacher nevertheless became a symbol of God's sensitivity to the enslaved. God used the slave preacher to articulate love, understanding, compassion, and strength through various modes of human characteristics—the former was certainly formed by the existential crisis of enslavement.

---

16. African American conceptual understanding of privilege, more often than not, is processed within a sociological understanding of race dynamics and cultural theory paradigms. Within American society, for instance, privilege is often attributed to whites due to their possession of wealth, positional social control, and majority racial status. The former formula is flawed in that it does not take into account the social stratification occurring within minority groups. Within the former, there exists an hierarchal dimension of a sub-group. Societal constructs are fluid—rarely is there an instance in which power and privilege are absent from the lived experiences of any race of people. Such was, and is, the case with African Americans.

17. Raboteau, *Slave Religion*, 233.

18. Ibid.

19. White, *The African Preacher*, 56.

20. Raboteau, *Slave Religion*, 233.

Existential Crisis of Enslavement

People often seek to locate meaning in times of existential crisis, a moment of bewilderment. When opposing worldviews collide, chaos often erupts; and out of this chaos, a perennial theme of cultural conflict emerges. When one's cosmological understanding is shattered, one becomes confused. The person who has made the conscious effort to live in a low-crime area, for instance, maneuvers in that particular world of comfort and security with limited concern regarding victimization. The prospect of becoming a victim may exist as a possibility, but to the uninitiated such an experience is improbable; that is, until it actually happens. The assailant views the potential victim as the *other* by negating the impact that such an experience potentially has on the human psyche. This *othering* stems from an assailant's desire to increase capital and establish a higher level of social ranking; even if such advancement is considered irrational from an opposing worldview. Any degree of advancement is significant within the assailants' distorted rationale. The victim, however, may begin to ponder existential concerns: Why did this happen to me? Will it happen again? How do I continue to lead a normal life after such a horrific ordeal? For some individuals engaged in existential crisis, everything is questioned when tragedy strikes, even God.

Mid-fifteenth-century Africans experienced such a cosmological collision with opportunistic Europeans. Africans were certainly familiar with the institutionalized concept of slavery. As an ideological component of warfare, conquered African peoples were relegated to serve at the behest of their African victors. Such were the spoils of war. But a European transition from feudalism to capitalism precipitated a philosophical difference in how both continents would approach a certain *pragmatics of slavery*. Although African slaves were accustomed to the reality of agricultural toil, they were unaccustomed to the dehumanizing work conditions of the Caribbean, West Indies, and North American plantation systems. Slave life expectancy in seventeenth-century Barbados, for instance, was a meager seventeen years.[21] Every African, regardless of social position, was vulnerable to European enslavement. Even African royalty (i.e., kings, queens, and princes) became victims of European avarice. "In 1526, Affonso, king of Kongo, wrote to Portugal complaining the 'there are many traders in all corners of the country. They bring ruin to the country. Every day people are

---

21. Frey and Wood, *Come Shouting to Zion*, 40.

enslaved and kidnapped, even nobles, even members of the king's family.'"[22] Religious figures of the African community were also captured, shipped, and sold to the higher bidder. The witch, medicine man, prophet, prophetess, diviner, rainmaker, and African priest were all a part of the cargo destined for the New World.

The existential crisis of this African and European collision must have caused a great deal of panic, fear, unsettlement, and confusion for the newly enslaved African. It is safe to assume they wondered why such a tragedy was happening to them. Naturally, these captured peoples would have resorted to a pattern of thinking that was ingrained in the African psyche (e.g., thoughts of freedom). African understanding of *self* would have presented many questions in relation to being thrust into a reality of perennial trauma, which was diametrically opposed to any of their previous experiences. Captured Africans would have processed that trauma and their consequent understanding of self on several levels.[23]

The first level would have entailed a socio-historical question regarding the ontological *self*. The captured Africans would have grappled existentially with being treated in such a manner. They also would have reflected on what, if any, personal acts had contributed to such a misfortune in this life and who they were as enslaved persons. The psychological awareness of *self*, however, would have prompted a defiant response to attempts at dehumanization. Akans' notion of *self*, for instance, included ancestors, community, personality spirit, siblings, spirits, God and Shadow (i.e., duality of self in the spiritual realm).[24] To be taken from one's community also entailed losing a sense of humanity, and would have prompted a need to re-define meaning within an existential state of meaninglessness. Captured Africans would also have anticipated some type of assistance from their ancestors for they believed that ancestors were intimately engaged in their destinies. If slavery was destined, what was the purpose? The awareness of self would also have been a foundational concern for religious leaders as they were responsible for interpreting any fundamental shift in African cosmology.

Patrick Manning and Peter Paris are correct in stating that the peoples of Africa did not possess a *unitary consciousness*.[25] After all, Africans had different religions, customs, and practices. But one must acknowledge

22. Nunn, "The Long-Term Effects of Africa's Slave Trades," 143.
23. Grills, "African Psychology," 195.
24. Ibid.
25. Paris, *The Spirituality of African Peoples*, 61.

that drastic cultural change also precipitates a shift in psychic adaptation. Something happened the moment enslaved Africans were shackled together and forced onto slave ships. They no longer had the cultural latitude to identify as static differentiated peoples. The goal of survival mandated that they attempt to discover commonality and put aside their animosities, diverse languages, and customs. The process of enslavement made them one: dynamic enslaved Africans. Yet Ira Berlin notes that solidarity among the enslaved was challenging as *conditions before the deck* prompted many to fight among themselves.[26] The captives, being confined to the storage areas onboard slave ships, began to compete for space in a reality that had been constructed by the slavers. "Tempers flared in the tight quarters, as the enslaved struggled among themselves for space, water, and food."[27] In times of protest and rebellion, some slaves actually preferred to align with the slavers as a means of survival; but the reality of their existential commonality of pain and suffering soon overcame such desires.

> Confederations born of shared anguish and pain made impossible situations more bearable, as captives bolstered each other's spirits, shared food, and nursed one another through bouts of nausea, fever, and dysentery. "I have seen them," reported one captain, "when their allowance happened to be short, divide the last morsel of meat amongst each other thread by thread." Small acts of kindness provided the basis for resistance, and a new order slowly took shape below deck. Sullen men and women began to forge a new language, from knowing gestures, a few shared words, and a desperate desire for human companionship. New languages—some of which had emerged from shared vocabularies of various African tongues and the common experience of African enslavement—gave birth to pidgins and then Creole languages. Men and women with an ear for language took the lead in this new multilingualism, and others soon followed, as the captives shared a need to communicate.[28]

It is psychologically beneficial to share stories of pain with people who have experienced the same or similar struggles. Sympathetic understanding provides a small sense of relief. Although fleeting, such an experience for the slave was enough to arouse the strength to survive the Middle Passage. And what a dreadful experience it was.

26. Berlin, *The Making of African America*, 65.
27. Ibid.
28. Ibid., 66.

After their capture, the Africans were tied together by a rope and then marched hundreds of miles while suffering from thirst, hunger, and exhaustion. Consequently, many either died along the way or were reduced to a very weak and emaciated condition by the time they reached the sea coast. On the coast, the Africans were made to jump up and down, had fingers poked in their mouths and their genital organs handled by the doctor. Those chosen by the Europeans were then branded. Taken on board ship, the naked Africans were shackled together on bare wooden boards in the hold, and packed so tightly that they could not sit upright. During the dreaded Mid-Passage (a trip of from three weeks to more than three months) the slaves were let out of the hold twice daily for meals and exercise, and women and children were often permitted to spend a great deal of time on deck. The foul and poisonous air of the hold, extreme heat, men lying for hours in their own defecation, with blood and mucus covering the floor, caused a great deal of sickness. Mortality from undernourishment and disease was about 16 per cent. The first few weeks of the trip was the most traumatic experience for the Africans. A number of them went insane and many became so despondent that they gave up the will to live. Slaves in the latter condition were described as having the "fixed melancholy." Africans were not, however, totally immobilized by shock. Often they committed suicide (especially while still on the African coast) by drowning, or refusing food or medicine, rather than accept enslavement.[29]

Captured Africans forged a new way of being in the early phase of slavery. African peoples became an African people. The survivors of the Middle Passage shared commonality in that peculiar experience, and as a result some survived. In addition, newly adapted African minds landed on shores of the New World. "On the Atlantic islands—Madeira, the Azores, the Canaries, and then Sao Tomé and Principe" the enslaved were introduced to "chattel bondage."[30] By the time of this introduction, it is quite probable that they were prepared for the experience. This is not to suggest that chattel slavery was an innocuous experience for the captives—it involved psychological and physical trauma beyond both human and divine understanding. But the exposure to the shock and trauma of the slave ship experience may have desensitized the captive to certain experiences of pain in the New World; be it by dissociation or any other coping mechanism, the

29. Blassingame, *The Slave Community*, 6–7.
30. Ibid., 54.

Mythical Meaning of the Slave Preacher

enslaved discovered a certain capacity that enabled their survival. Among this group of survivors emerged the slave preacher.

Scholars contend that the "original, full-fledged, unique type of Negro preaching in America [*old-time and old-fashioned*]" commenced in 1732.[31] This contention takes into account the use of Christian missionization among the enslaved as experienced in the First Great Awakening. Slave preaching, however, commenced the moment enslaved Africans presented a unified moan to the ancestors via priests and other religious interpreters. James Weldon Johnson argues that, "it was through him that the people of diverse languages and customs who were brought here from diverse parts of Africa and thrown into slavery were given their first sense of unity and solidarity. He was the first shepherd of this bewildered flock."[32] The reputation of such religious interpreters was certainly retained outside of the African geographical location.[33] Ritualistic procedures for interpreting phenomena were also at their disposal.[34] But who would become the sole religious leader amidst many religious figures? This negotiation eventually led to the formation and role of the slave preacher. According to Gayraud Wilmore:

> We do know that many of the early underground preachers to the slaves were not white men, but African priests who possessed unusual gifts of leadership and persuasion. One known source of such leaders was Dahomey, where dynastic quarrels produced persons who were then sold to white traders as slaves. Some of the victims were not only the defeated chiefs and their families, but also his priests and among the people conquered by the Dahomeans were the local priests of the river cults.[35]

Just as the priest was a prominent figure in Africa, the slave preacher became the premiere religious agent within the slave community. Slave preachers had the power and ability to establish and reiterate cultural norms that more or less governed the identity of the community. The slave preacher also assisted in the construction of a new religious system. This

---

31. Pipes, *Say Amen, Brother!*, 7; Mitchell, *Black Preaching*, 32. Albert J. Raboteau contends that the slave preacher began "exercising his gift" around 1770. See Raboteau, "Introduction," in Johnson, *God Struck Me Dead*, xxi.

32. Johnson, *God's Trombones*, 2.

33. Frey and Wood, *Come Shouting to Zion*, 56.

34. Chireau, *Black Magic*, 41.

35. Wilmore, *Black Religion and Black Radicalism*, 8.

system aided in the communal survival of an oppressed people seeking mental and physical respite as "slaves were beaten, chained, incarcerated, ironed, and whipped; and they watched as their wives, husbands, mothers, fathers, children, and relatives were flogged."[36] However, some slave preachers advanced the agenda of the master and mistress as a means of personally securing a better lot within the suffocating world of slavery. One such example is Jupiter Hammon, who had a reputation for articulating a paternalistic theology in his sermons to slaves.

> Here is a plain command of God for us to obey our masters. It may seem hard for us, if we think our masters wrong in holding us slaves, to obey in all things, but who of us dare dispute with God! He has commanded us to obey, and we ought to do it cheerfully, and freely. This should be done by us, not only because God commands, but because our own peace and comfort depend upon it. As we depend upon our maters, for what we eat and drink and wear, and for all our comfortable things in this world, we cannot be happy, unless we please them.[37]

As leaders of the community, slave preachers were aware of conversation among its members regarding rebellion and escape. Understandably, "tens of thousands of blacks each year demonstrated their discontent by going on the run."[38] Slave preachers had the power to contribute to the cause of freedom by becoming double agents (e.g., they could pretend to be working against the community on the one hand, and on the other, provide misinformation as a means to mislead the slave masters), or they could alert the master about various plots being mulled over in the slave community. This latter type of preacher within the slave community has been identified as the *parasitic* type.[39] Although there are several instances in which some slave preachers worked against the slave community, it was an atypical phenomenon when one considers the broad scope of slave preachers who actually endured additional suffering for their fellow slaves. Although the slave preacher is often discussed in terms of preaching prowess, adroitness, and community influence, I take a much broader approach to appreciate fully the psychological resolve, genius, and communal commitment that is displayed in the personhood of the slave preacher. Within such

36. Franklin and Schweninger, *Runaway Slaves*, 42.
37. Hammon, "Address to the Negroes in the State of New York," 34–43.
38. Franklin and Schweninger, *Runaway Slaves*, 48.
39. Hicks, *Images of the Black Preacher*, 30.

an analytical context, how the slave preacher experienced and understood conversion is of vital concern. For it is during the conversion experience that God is defined as an *Aid* for the downtrodden.

Although conversion entailed a type of spiritual transformation, slave conversion must be treated as a different paradigm, for the Christian religion initially complicated rather than complimented the slaves' traumatic notions of religious and spiritual life. Neglecting to address this convoluted gap is what has garnered the slave preacher a certain mystique. The myth or symbolism associated with the slave preachers' ontology is of paramount concern as it indicates its generational transmission and dependability, but such an experience is compounded as the slave preacher grappled with personal trauma, the collective trauma of the community, and the overwhelming burden of living up to the standard of leadership that was formed in the belly of the slave ship. To understand the slave preacher then, we must first understand slave trauma.

Slave Trauma

Trauma is a mental state in which human beings grapple with and respond to both conscious and unconscious thoughts regarding events and experiences that exposed them to potential death and/or serious injury. In her book *Trauma and Recovery*, Judith Herman posits that it is normal in such situations to repress *atrocities* within consciousness; however, such an attempt is futile, as some human experiences are situated perennially as memories of torment.[40] Repression of painful experiences is often accomplished by believing that intentional forgetfulness renders painful experiences ineffective. This type of response is normal as discussing a traumatic experience makes a person re-experience pain and tragedy. Even if one consciously succeeds in choosing to forget, more often than not, such memories are unconsciously activated via "nightmares and unnamed anxieties."[41] Nancy Howard, a slave from Maryland, "reported that she was frequently punished by raw hides, was hit with tongs and poker and anything. 'I used when I went out, to look up at the sky, and say, Blessed Lord, oh, do take me out of this!' It seemed to me I could not bear another lick. I can't forget it. I sometimes dream that I am pursued, and when I wake, I am scared

---

40. Herman, *Trauma and Recovery*, 1.
41. Jones, *Trauma and Grace*, 78.

almost to death.'"[42] Regardless of the method of activation and presentation, trauma has the capacity to alter the make-up of the human anatomy, particularly the psyche.[43] Group trauma is often referred to as cultural trauma. Jeffery C. Alexander explains that in order for trauma to be classified as a culturally grouped phenomenon, "social crises must become cultural crises. Events are one thing; representations of these events are quite another. Trauma is not the result of a group experiencing pain. It is the result of this acute discomfort entering into the core of the collectivity's sense of its own identity." Collective actors *decide* to represent social pain as a fundamental threat to their sense of who they are, where they came from, and where they want to go.[44] The traumatized group, then, identifies cultural trauma as a phenomenon that has defined their past, present, and future. Alexander further posits that the traumatized group must first ascertain the nature of said pain.[45] In other words, there is a shared experience of trauma that resides as a bonding cultural phenomenon for a particular social group. Although each individual within the social group processes this experience internally and separately, commonality associated with a specific traumatic experience creates a defined way of existing or being as a group. Common lived experiences such as cultural trauma may also become normalized due to the dominant or pervasive nature of the shared experience.

Joy DeGruy, in *Post Traumatic Slave Syndrome,* suggests that psychological and physical trauma associated with being enslaved and with purposeful intentions by slave owners to harm, generationally transmitted notions of inferiority and anxiety to slave descendants. She asserts, "slavery yielded stressors that were both disturbing and traumatic, exacting a wound upon the African American psyche which continues to fester."[46] When punishment became too severe, some "slaves mutilated themselves or committed suicide rather than submit to painful floggings;"[47] additionally, "the hopelessness of slavery occasionally caused mental illness in the quarters and led to the inclusion of bondsmen among the insane and idiotic persons enumerated in the United States censuses."[48] But one of the

42. Blassingame, *The Slave Community*, 302.
43. Van der Kolk, *The Body Keeps Score*, 82.
44. Alexander, *Trauma*, 15.
45. Ibid., 17–19.
46. DeGruy, *Post Traumatic Slave Syndrome*, 112.
47. Ibid., 296.
48. Ibid., 298.

greatest causes of mental issue, according to Blassingame, was the "separation of family members."⁴⁹ The traumatic experience of slavery affected both primary (i.e., actual slaves) and secondary (i.e., descendants of slaves) cultural agents of the African American experience. Slave traumatization created a mode of existence in which the enslaved obtained learned patterns of cultural and relational behavior. James H. Sweet notes "there were also slaves who, as adults, repeated the patterns of violence and abuse that were carried out against them as children."⁵⁰

Some slaves were socially conditioned to interpret violence as a normal means of voicing discontent, but this trait was not confined simply to the protest against white slave masters; *fellow slaves*⁵¹ were also victims of violent protests, as the traumatized enslaved psyche could not differentiate cultural variations of aggression. According to C. G. Jung:

> Psychology teaches us that, in a certain sense, there is nothing in the psyche that is old; nothing that can really, definitively die away. Even Paul was left with a sting in his flesh. Whoever protects himself against what is new and strange and thereby regresses to the past, falls into the same neurotic condition as the man who identifies himself with the new and runs away from the past. The only difference is that the one has estranged himself from the past, and the other from the future. In principle both are doing the same thing; they are salvaging a narrow state of consciousness. The alternative is to shatter it with the tension inherent in the play of opposites—in the dualistic stage—and thereby to build up a state of wider and higher consciousness.⁵²

The process of African enslavement created a psychological space of consciousness that influenced the external worlds of slaves on a daily basis. In this experience of consciousness, it would have been difficult for enslaved persons to process aggression at a high level of awareness. For the enslaved, acts of aggression were merely modes of cathartic expressions of pain. The victims of this experience were casualties of psychological trauma. This is the result whenever groups of oppressed people have limited outlets of functional emotional expression. For Jung, the dualistic stage of higher consciousness entails the ability to be psychologically positioned between

---

49. Ibid., 299.
50. Sweet, *Recreating Africa*, 81.
51. Ibid.
52. Jung, *Modern Man in Search of a Soul*, 102.

the realities of the past and the future; while existing in the here-and-now, one possesses the ability to exist in a conscious state of potentiality. However, it is important to note that Jung's higher consciousness coincided with positively relating to a westernized understanding of past, present, and future time. The inability to process European conceptual past, present, and future time could have altered how African consciousness would come to process the lived experience of enslavement, thus affecting the psyche.

African notions of time consisted of the long past, the present, and no real future. John Mbiti uses the Swahili words Sasa and Zamani[53] to differentiate African notions of time from European ones. Sasa means here and now; thus for Mbiti, Sasa "is the period of immediate concern for the people, since that is where or when they exist."[54] This time would have been important to enslaved Africans as it illuminated acts of torture, rape, murder, beatings, and so on within a time category that defined the most meaningful experience for traditional Africans. The philosophical appeal for existential meaning is therefore valid in that "Sasa is the most meaningful period for the individual."[55] This cosmological shift in experience no doubt caused many to panic as existential meaning was reduced to that of trauma. Moreover, a group of captured slaves would suffer more than the captured individual as "the community has its own Sasa, which is greater than that of the individual."[56] Zamani also has its own past, present and future.[57] The African past is different from the European concept of past in that traditional African thought treats the past as endless. African history moves backward, "because time has no end."[58] For the West African, history is endless because there is a rhythmic pattern from the Sasa to the Zamani. Forcibly removing Africans, therefore, from their geographical location is a disruption of their rhythmic Sasa and Zamani. Because the land "is an expression of this Sasa and Zamani,"[59] enslaved Africans were willing to die as they knew no other existence beyond the current experience of slavery (Sasa and Zamani) time. The traumatic disruption of time and space caused many Africans to attempt suicide.

53. Mbiti, *African Religions and Philosophy*, 21.
54. Ibid.
55. Ibid., 22.
56 Ibid.
57 Ibid.
58 Ibid., 23.
59 Ibid.

Mythical Meaning of the Slave Preacher

But like so much of our singing and dancing at white command ever since, the activity was not primarily for our benefit or entertainment, but for white profits, ordered because dancing was considered therapeutic, was supposed to ensure us against the "melancholy" that drove countless thousands of Africans to suicide in the course of the middle passage.[60]

As the Israelites[61] were required to entertain their Babylonian captives with song, the African slaves were also required "to sing, and they sang songs of sorrow. Their sickness, fear of being beaten, their hunger, and the memory of their country are the usual subjects. Then late at night, after the songs were over, from the darkness of the lower decks of the *Young Hero* and a thousand other ships, the sailors often could hear an howling melancholy noise, expressive of extreme anguish."[62] Frantz Fanon is correct in stating that the act of dehumanization causes the colonized to question who they are in light of the new experience of oppression.[63] The captured African developed an abbreviated consciousness that retained components of self-worth and dignity, but the social condition[64] of enslavement forced the captives to re-imagine freedom and liberation; not in terms of African existence as was known within a pre-slavery context, but in terms of how African freedom should be retained and imagined in the here-and-now moment of enslavement.

The experience of trauma, according to Stanley Elkins, rendered the slave psychologically void and detached. He further suggests that slaves encountered several shocks from the slave experience.[65] Blassingame's treatment of the Middle Passage *shock* differs, however, from Elkins' view. The

---

60 Harding, *There is a River*, 16.

61. In the postexilic era, Ibn Ezra provides an account of psychological angst associated with being taken away from the religious/cultural symbol (i.e., the Temple) that identified their association with God. The captives wept as they considered the social implication of the destruction of the temple. Devoid of their religious heritage, they "sat and wept as they thought of Zion." To add insult to this injury, the Babylonians, "our tormentors" demanded that the Israelites, in their captive state, sing songs that could only be appreciated as significant within the culture milieu of Temple worship. Ibn Ezra states that the Israelites refused to sing meaningful songs in a place foreign to their religious and cultural heritage. See (Psalm 137:1–4) Berlin and Brettler, eds., *The Jewish Study Bible*, 1424.

62. Ibid.

63. Frantz Fanon, *The Wretched of the Earth*, 182.

64. Birt, *Existence, Identity and Liberation*, 211.

65. Elkins, *Slavery*, 99–101.

first phase of enslavement (i.e., capture, the march, jail, medical inspection, branding, and the ship hold) entailed an horrific experience, but the shock was not enough to eradicate the enslaved Africans' ability to reason cosmologically. It was logically reasonable, according to Blassingame, for the enslaved African to consider suicide as an act of protest. It was a means to rid the enslaved of the experience of trauma, and return them to the collective memory of their ancestral past. For Elkins, suicide was an act of life resignation; the enslaved Africans, however, envisioned suicide to be a means by which they transitioned spiritually into a new state of blissful African existence. While discussing the relatively high percentage of slave suicides and identifying that "the shock of enslavement was crucial in determining their behavior,"[66] Blassingame alludes to an abbreviated comparison between the African American experience in chattel slavery to that of other experiences "in such total institutions as concentration camps, prisons, and armies."[67] Elkins, on the other hand, unequivocally correlates the physical and psychological experience of African American enslavement with that of Jewish Holocaust victims. Elkins suggests that Jews adjusted to absolute power in Nazi concentration camps; yet no matter the degree of their resistance, the brutality of the Nazi Germans resulted in the construction of a passive and submissive Jewish personality. He locates this same personality type within the enslaved African experience. Blassingame's treatment of the slave personality is far more nuanced. For instance, he contends such an experience entailed being manipulated in every regard by *non-members* of the group within a total institution. The cruel treatment (e.g., starvation, daily torture, and murder) that concentration camp inmates received caused them to be extremely submissive, infantile, and docile. A much *milder* treatment, however, "led [prisoners] to be deferential toward their superordinates while rejecting their norms and participating in underground resistance to them."[68]

The first shock was that of capture, a capture quite unlike one the enslaved might have known through previous intertribal wars. For even if the defeated party became subjugated, there remained an attachment to the ancestors and deities, to nature and family. Through nature, one had a sense of being cared for by ancestors who experienced a new existence as an animal or another natural phenomenon. The living dead were also important to the African (as long as the name of the relative remained active in the

---

66. Blassingame, *The Slave Community*, 13.
67. Ibid., 290.
68. Ibid.

Mythical Meaning of the Slave Preacher

hearts and minds of the community). It was vitally important for Africans to stay connected, if for no other reason than to remind people constantly of the living dead. Such dedication ensured that the deceased would remain with them and not depart and join the ancestors. The social rupture that European capture caused is what created discontent and trauma in the heart of the newly enslaved. Being disconnected from the community was something heretofore unfathomable to them.

Elkins also posited that "hardships, thirst, brutalities, and near starvation penetrated the experience of each exhausted man and woman who reached the coast."[69] Thomas Fowell Buxton first treated this issue of the *death march*[70] in 1839.[71] The march to the sea was progressive in nature. Several factors determined the morality rate among slaves. For instance, "distance, diet, disease, and amount of cargo carried"[72] all factored into the degree to which captured Africans suffered. Early mortality rates indicated "that 50 percent of all those intended for transatlantic markets died during seizure, march, and detention."[73] Captured Africans who survived the march were soon branded as a means of identifying them as property of their newly acquired owner. This unique process of identifying human property is known to us from earlier enslavement by Babylonia. Then, the branding read: "I am his slave."[74]

The shock of the Middle Passage produced psychological horror for the enslaved. The two month trek across the Atlantic left the slave with little hope, and with much despair. Benjamin G. Brawley notes that

> Sometimes there were stern fights on board. Sometimes food was refused in order that death might be hastened. When opportunity served, some leaped overboard in the hope of being taken back to Africa. Throughout the night the hold resounded with the moans of those who awoke from dreams of home to find themselves in bonds. Women became hysterical, and both men and women

---

69. Ibid., 99.

70. Ira Berlin declares, "Conditions improved over time, but in the 1790s one in four slaves taken in central Africa died before reaching the coast. In some places, more than half the slaves perished between their initial capture in the interior and their arrival on the coast. Overall, the movement to the coast was nothing more than a death march for many." See Berlin, *The Making of African America*, 56.

71. See Klein et al., "Transoceanic Mortality," 93–118.

72. Ibid.

73. Ibid.

74. Johnson, *Branded*, 231.

became insane. Fearful and contagious diseases broke out. Smallpox was one of these. More common was ophthalmia, a frightful inflammation of the eyes. A blind, and hence worthless, slave was thrown to the sharks.[75]

Regarding dietary rations for the Middle Passage, according to John Thornton, "slaves were fed only once in every twenty-four hours." This meal consisted of "a medium-sized bowl of corn millet flour or raw millet gruel."[76] During the Atlantic trek, dehydration was also a constant issue as many Africans suffered from seasickness "and vomited frequently."[77] The epidemic of diarrhea onboard slave ships was prevalent as a result of the new diet. Additionally, slaves often disembarked the slave vessels with potentially life threatening diseases such as typhoid fever, measles, yellow fever, and smallpox, as evidenced in Brazil in 1616 and 1617.[78]

The final shock was that of so-called seasoning. This process entailed the newly enslaved Africans becoming accustomed to a new language, culture, and the Christian God. The more they were inundated with notions of Americanization, the less likely, it was hoped, they were to cling to the cultural norms of their African heritage. "Actually," according to Elkins, "a great deal had happened to him already. Much of his past had been annihilated; nearly every prior connection had his family and kinship arrangements, his language, the tribal religion, the taboos, the name he had once borne, and so on—but none of it any longer carried much meaning."[79] Cultural meaning and memory of slave trauma, as seen in transgenerational epigenetic inheritance, substantiates the claim that traumatic experiences can have such a negative effect on the human psyche that suffering becomes encoded in human DNA, passed down to future generations.[80] Peter L. Levine "strongly suspects that many African Americans are still suffering from the residual dark cloud drifting ominously behind the eradication of slavery. In fact, the lack of adequate educational opportunities in US ghettos today,

---

75. Brawley, *A Social History of the American Negro*, 19.

76. Thornton, *Africa and Africans*, 155–56.

77. Ibid., 157.

78. Ibid.

79. Elkins, *Slavery*, 10.

80. See Yehuda et al., "Holocaust Exposure"; Van der Kolk, *The Body Keeps the Score*, 75–103; Berry et al., *Cross-Cultural Psychology*, 107; Levine, *Trauma and Memory*; Janice A. Walters, "Trauma and Resilience among a Stolen Generation of Indigenous People" in O' Loughlin and Charles, *Fragments of Trauma*.

as well as the subjugation and mass incarcerations of millions of black men and boys, reinforces this tragic legacy of generational trauma."[81]

Elkins and Blassingame are correct in their analyses of the psychological trauma associated with the trans-Atlantic process of enslavement. However, as other scholars have noted, Elkins overdoes his point regarding how the traumatic process of slavery left the enslaved totally devoid of their African cultural roots and meanings and utterly submissive to the norms of the institution of chattel slavery. To be sure, slaves endured a huge psychological and cultural shock that left them seeking meaning in a meaninglessness situation; but even if the experience of slavery left them devoid of meaning in a state of slave existence, they nevertheless retained the psychic capacity to create a generationally established cultural memory and African identity within a New World.

Blassingame disagrees with Elkins' comparative conclusion regarding Jewish Holocaust prisoners and the African American experience with plantation slavery. By referring to interpersonal psychology and his understanding of total institutions, Blassingame concludes that Nazi operatives, under the influence of twentieth-century scientific research, employed tactics and strategies that similarly had proven effective in making human beings infantile, docile, and submissive. The slave masters, however, were not interested in annihilating their slaves. Although beatings, rape, and murder were common within the plantation system, slave owners were interested in profit, not the extermination of a race of people. Blassingame does acknowledge that plantation and holocaust survivors share an experience in that they "maintained their psychical balance because of group solidarity," had "prior experience in similar institutions," reflected on "religious ideals," experienced "a culture differing greatly from that of their oppressors," had "prior referents for self-esteem," and "possessed a degree of physical stamina."[82]

The Negotiated Slave Preacher

Despite all these enormous privations and traumas, the African priest nevertheless remained a religious symbol in the New World. As would be the case in Africa, the enslaved looked to their religious symbol for a

---

81. Levine, *Trauma and Memory*, 164.
82. Blassingame, *The Slave Community*, 331.

sign—wondering about some divine rationale for their current plight.[83] African priesthood as aligned in familial hereditary, entailing both men and women,[84] would perform religious rituals on behalf of the community. The New World African priesthood, devoid of established lineages of the office, soon became accessible to "anyone who performs religious duties."[85] Attempting to maintain a sense of order amidst a chaotic experience, it is possible that slaves possibly designated a religious leader based on who had retained the most information regarding familiar religious rituals and ceremonies. Early in the transportation phase, "in slave communities from the Caribbean to Brazil, African people carried the rituals, theological principles, and liturgical practices of their ancestors into new environments. Slave religious traditions were supplemented with alternative practices and beliefs, some extracted from non-African sources."[86] Du Bois argues, however, that official African priests, second only to the chief, did indeed function as the first slave preachers, in that they attempted to provide a cosmological understanding for their current lived experience.

> His realm alone—the province of religion and medicine—remained largely unaffected by the plantation system in many important particulars. The Negro priest, therefore, early became an important figure on the plantation and found his function as the interpreter of the supernatural, the comforter of the sorrowing, and as the one who expressed, rudely, but picturesquely, the longing and disappointment and resentment of a stolen people.[87]

Blassingame contends that *the early spiritual leaders* were representatives of traditional African religions. It was these slave preachers who preached "the efficacy of the spirit world and the protecting gods of their homeland" to the people.[88] Henry T. Mitchell suggests that the early attempt to regulate slave gatherings is a clear indication that their New World system had bonded many forms of traditional African religious practices.[89] Such togetherness can be seen in the negotiation between the African sorcerer and priest. Du Bois contends that the destruction of the office of the

---

83. Parrinder, *Religion in Africa*, 54.
84. Mbiti, *African Religions and Philosophy*, 183.
85. Ibid., 182.
86. Chireau, *Black Magic*, 41.
87. Du Bois, *The Negro Church*, 24.
88. Blassingame, *The Slave Community*, 24–25.
89. Mitchell, *Black Church Beginnings*, 24.

Mythical Meaning of the Slave Preacher

African priest provided opportunity for an unchallenged process in which some took on priestly roles and functions; as a result, a mixture of "African religion and witchcraft appeared in the West Indies, which was known as Obi."[90] Leonard Barrett notes that the DuBoisian *Obi* has the same root as the Ashanti word *Obeah*, which indicates a practitioner of witchcraft.

> It is a combination of three words: *oba*, a child; *yi*, to take away; and *fo*, he who. The root meaning of the combined words yields: he who takes a child away. This simply supports the theory in witchcraft literature that the final test for one to enter into the fraternity of sorcerers is the sacrifice of a child, either his own or that of a relative.[91]

The Obeahman was an early leader for the slave community. In fact, Cuffy, "the leader of a 1675 Barbados insurrection, is thought to have been an Obeahman."[92] The slaves' New World was traumatic, confusing, and chaotic. Legitimate priests attempted to address this chaotic world using their limited authority; because they were no longer connected to the source of their powers, they soon discovered that traditional ways of addressing their current dilemma would be unsuccessful. The sorcerer, on the other hand, was somewhat familiar with using dubious tactics to remedy social ills. Therefore, the priest, "powerless and equally knowledgeable in the techniques of sorcery, joined forces with the sorcerer in the unleashing of the psychic forces against the common enemy."[93] The negotiation between the sorcerer and the African priest was a means of survival and produced a unified slave preacher. To be sure, the sorcerer and priest differed in regards to notions of religious practices, but they joined powers and prepared for further development as they began to understand that conversion language was liberative in nature. By the eighteenth century, Obeah was a known leader among the slaves "in all plantation colonies."[94]

This example of adaptation endorses Viktor Frankl's notion that it is a central theme in life.[95] Slaves learned to adapt to their situation. They changed themselves. Although adaptation entailed some acquiescence on the part of slaves, they never adopted every tenet of white-slave holding

---

90. Du Bois, *The Negro Church*, 24.
91. Barrett, *Soul Force*, 64.
92. Gerbner, *Christian Slavery*, 98.
93. Barrett, *Soul Force*, 65.
94. Frey and Wood, *Come Shouting to Zion*, 57.
95. Frankl, *Man's Search for Meaning*, 135.

Christianity. The majority of slaves understood enslavement to be morally unjustifiable. The slave preacher, as the moral leader of the community, reiterated this notion by contradicting sermons that sought to construct blacks as subservient and *other*. The slaves' newly deconstructed view of God provided glimpses of hope, promise, and meaning.

Meaning and Conversion

For nearly three hundred years, the slave preacher [Obeahman] sought to define meaning and purpose for the slave community via acts of rebellion, poisonings,[96] and ritualistic interpretations. This period, in my estimation, was a period in which the slave preacher struggled to remain true to the religious traditions of the past. I presume that the slave preacher initially combated the *gods* of the white man with a sense of confidence, but the constant influx of slaves must have left the slave preacher suffering like Sisyphus. *The negotiation* that the slave preacher modeled was an early indication that survival was of the utmost concern. If the enslaved desired a more thriving position in life, they would need to rely upon more than just defensive tactics that early slave preaching proposed; they would need to develop an offensive strategy that would create meaning and purpose in their lives, despite being enslaved. This, of course, is not to argue that slaves were devoid of meaning in their lives prior to their Christianization. The collision with European powers created a context in which adaptation seemed sensible for the African priest and sorcerer; now the descendants of this merger would also have to adapt to some religious notions of their capturers, while at the same time creating a new religion that would instill meaning within the souls of a newly grafted people.

For the slave, conversion was a transformation in consciousness.[97] The slave entered a supernatural realm and became transfixed with the power of the Christian God. One slave recalls being engaged in the activity of dancing; but upon falling asleep, "I felt so wicked. I laid and prayed, and while I lay there the prettiest music came to me. I told the Lord I wanted to see where the music came from, and I looked above me and saw many angels and heard the flapping of their wings."[98] A slave was also confronted with personal sin; as a result, the slave entered a realm of regeneration—a

96. Frey and Wood, *Come Shouting to Zion*, 61.
97. Raboteau, "Introduction," xx.
98. Johnson, *God Struck Me Dead*, 124.

Mythical Meaning of the Slave Preacher

supernatural space which provided power to combat the ills of slave existence. Through conversion, God empowered the slave to *fight on anyhow*.

Whites promoted slave conversion largely to subdue the spirit of the *heathen*. Black Touchstone, in describing notions of Christianity in the south, posited that "The majority of planters at the Charleston meeting firmly believed that the conversion of slaves would do much more than save black souls."[99] The white southern slave owner used Christianity as a tool to control slave behavior by "encouraging slaves to be honest and diligent laborers, promote public safety by checking or diverting the passions of blacks, and refute abolitionist criticism by demonstrating that slavery in the South was a Christian institution."[100] Paul Radin understands slave conversion to entail a negotiation reminiscent of the sorcerer and the African priest; this negotiation was more pronounced as slaves reasoned that the power source of their slave masters could only be obtained through the specific ritual of the conversion experience. African American slaves, therefore, sought to possess some of the power that had been controlling their lives for nearly three hundred years. This conscious striving for a more balanced universe led to an attractiveness for the Christian religion.[101]

Slave conversion was often a sensuous experience. Riggins Earl contends that "all claimants of the authentic conversion experience must have: "felt the power of God"; "seen the travail of his or her soul"; and "tasted the love of God."[102] For the slave, being *struck dead* entailed a psychological passage in which the slave entered dream consciousness.[103] This realm was a place where God communed with the slave; reassured the slave of self-worth, and empowered the slave to exist in a dialectical state of spiritual bliss/physical anguish. As articulated by one slave preacher, "There is a man in man. The soul is the medium between God and man. God speaks to us through our conscience, and the reasoning is so loud that we seem to hear a voice. But if God gave us the power of speech, can he not talk? If a soul calls on God, having no other earthly hope, will God not reveal himself."[104]

White preaching held little interest to the enslaved in the mid-eighteenth century. And no wonder, for compared to the African religious

---

99. Touchstone, "Planters and Slave Religion," 101.
100. Ibid.
101. Radin, "Foreword," viii–ix.
102. Earl, *Dark Symbols, Obscure Signs*, 52.
103. Ibid., 53.
104. Johnson, *God Struck Me Dead*, 14.

tradition of orality, dance, music, and songs, Christian religion was stifling, boring, and hypocritical. Nevertheless, during the fifteenth century, France and Spain, being Catholic countries, sought to convert the African *heathen* to Christianity (although Native Americans were the first group to undergo conversion attempts). During the 1630s, a great deal of debate ensued regarding whether African American slaves could or should be brought into the Christian faith. However, by 1667 Virginia State law had settled the issue by declaring baptism does not alter the condition of the enslaved. Founded by Thomas Bray in 1701, The Society for the Propagation of the Gospel (SPG), which was an Anglican Missionary Organization, was mainly focused on the premise of morality. It was responsible for some conversions in the Carolinas, Pennsylvania, New York, and New Jersey. Overall, SPG efforts of slave conversion were unsuccessful. The Catholics also experienced meager success due to their smaller denomination and the rivalry between Catholic immigrants and blacks. Additionally, they did not care for bringing blacks into their worship spaces. They lacked sufficient clergy and worship locations to accommodate their vision. Ultimately, their religious formalism was not appealing to blacks. In 1706, Cotton Mather published *The Negro Christianized: An Essay to Excite and Assist that Good Work, the Instruction of Negro-Servants in Christianity*. Mather proposed that slave owners were obligated to educate their Negro servants in the Christian religion, to treat them humanely, and to accept them as spiritual brethren.

Anglicans failed because of a shortage of missionaries. Anglicans also demanded for slaves to know the Catechism perfectly. Anglican Church's religious instruction, therefore, required a lot of time, time that slaves did not have. Moreover, slaves were incapable of grasping the Anglican tenets of faith—not for lack of intelligence but because it was a herculean task to learn a language and a new religion simultaneously, in addition to being enslaved. The low conversion during the colonial period were largely due to the Africans' preference for their own African-based beliefs and practices, which were kept alive by the newly arriving shipments of Africans.

When the First Great Awakening occurred in the 1730s and 1740s, the focus was on conversion of natives, slaves, and colonists. In this period, George Whitefield[105] began a preaching campaign in and through colonial

---

105. Many mid-eighteenth century New England preachers viewed *The Great Awakening* of slave conversion as an uncouth mockery of an otherwise serious and civilized spiritual experience; but to the enslaved, nothing could have been further from the truth. In fact, slave conversion was civilized in the sense that African religious traditionalists understood spirit possession to entail an experience in which the possessed relinquished

America. Whitefield, like many white clergy in the eighteenth century, believed that blacks could remain slaves while also being spiritually liberated. In fact, that "Whitefield was interested personally in owning slaves actually appears as early as December, 1741."[106] His elitist attitude toward white privilege and belief of black savagery "was an indication of his conviction that the doctrine of regeneration was the most important of all the doctrines of Christianity."[107] Nevertheless, Whitefield's departure from the old way of communicating God's word (i.e., via manuscript renderings in closed buildings that were often inaccessible to slaves) to a new extemporaneous style in the open field became attractive to slaves. The tonality of Whitefield's preaching was also akin to the West African griots' presentation of heroic material, imagery, and metrical pattern.[108]

This new form of evangelism,[109] according to Donald Mathews, "brought God down from His Aloofness into human life in a most dramatic and personal way which no reason could deny."[110] Moreover, Whitefield's use of word pictures would have connected to the slaves in imaginative ways. Whitefield proclaimed on one occasion, "Oh, let there be joy in heaven over some of you repenting! Though we are in a field, I am persuaded

---

control, as the possessing Spirit controlled the body, mind, and soul of the possessed. George Whitefield, although subject to the racist culture in which he lived, was the proverbial bridge that would escort many slaves to Christ via his fiery and emotional sermons. Whitefield provided the slaves with a context of adaptable religious potentiality. West African culture entailed a degree of emotional expression. Africans were accustomed to dancing, jumping, shouting, spirit possession, orality, and so on. William H. Pipes concludes that "Whitefield's emotional preaching did more, perhaps, than anything else to encourage the slave along the road of mental escape from his conditions." Additionally, Whitefield was successful among the slaves due to several preaching elements: 1) He was of decent height. 2) "Perfect voice modulation." 3) He had a flare for "dramatics." 4) He possessed a vivid imagination. 5) He was persuasive. 6) He preached without a manuscript. See Pipes, *Say Amen, Brother!*, 61 and Lambert, "I Saw the Book Talk," 12.

106. Sloat, "George Whitefield," 7.

107. Ibid., 12.

108. Simmons, "Whooping," 867.

109. The first Evangelical Revivals produced two major denominations: the Baptist and Methodist. Slaves reacted to these denominations in positive ways. For instance, slave affinity toward Baptist and Methodist faith traditions had a slow appeal due to the late start in conversion endeavors within the colonial system. Nevertheless, they appealed to the mind of slaves and the way they worshiped. The Evangelical style and ethos 1) were of biblically-based preaching, 2) included particular engaging teaching mechanisms (e.g., Sunday School/Preaching) and 3) gave blacks more freedom to preach.

110. Mathews, *Religion in the Old South*, 13.

the blessed angels are hovering now around us, and do long, "as the hart panteth after the waterbrooks," to sing an anthem at your conversion."[111] He declared that "nearly fifty negroes came to give me thanks for what God had done to their souls."[112] On another occasion, he stated that "I believe masters and mistresses will shortly see that Christianity will not make their Negroes worse slaves."[113] Whitefield substantiates the claim that slave conversion was progressive in nature; though they might desire to know God, the slave could not force the movement of God; but when the event occurred, it was often illustrated through emotional release in dance, song, tears, and shouts. Slave conversion became the fruitful evidence that one had been struck dead by God, as Whitefield describes:

> I conversed also with a poor Negro Woman, who has been in a very remarkable manner. God was pleased to convert her by my preaching last autumn; but being under dejections on Sunday morning, she prayed that salvation might come to her heart, and that the Lord would be pleased to manifest Himself to her soul that day. Whilst she was meeting, hearing Mr. M......n, a Baptist preacher, the Word came with such power to her heart, that at last she was obliged to cry out; and a great concern fell upon many in the congregation. The minister stopped, and several persuaded her to hold her peace; but she could not help praising and blessing God.[114]

Conversion provided meaning for the slaves in various ways, and the slave preacher understood this best, as he was the one who knew intimately and extensively the depth and breadth of being owned by God rather than by human beings. With this understanding, the slave preacher developed a new way in which to interpret life. The slave was no longer a fleeting thought in the mind of the Christian God. Moreover, God indeed cared about the suffering of slaves, and provided a spiritual realm that could only be obtained through the individual psyche. Because African notions of religion are communally based, the onus was upon the converted slave to provide evidence of this new creation in God, and with this testimony was

---

111. Whitefield, *Sermons of George Whitefield*, 97.
112. Whitefield, *George Whitefield Journals*, 422.
113. Ibid.
114. Ibid., 419–20.

received into a new life within a new community of spiritually liberated African Americans.

The early shock and traumatic experience of enslaved Africans forged in them a mental and spiritual desire to be free. The slave preacher, with limited power, soon discovered that mythological language and Christian folklore was similar to the African ethos of meaningful story telling. The exodus narrative, Jesus and his struggle with death, Moses and the Hebrews all conveyed that God also wanted slaves to be physically free, and this could be accomplished by accessing the power of the Christian God. Whereas the slaver preacher furthered his eminence within the community, the slave preacher used mythological persuasion and the slave experience to create a more pronounced existence for slaves via story telling.

Myth, Meaning, and the Slave Preacher

Mythology is a poetic expression of meaning. More often than not, myth is communicated through speech.[115] Myths obtain ontological essence, according to G. Van Der Leeuw, by being "repeatedly spoken anew."[116] Myths, because they are "replete with power,"[117] also assist people in interpreting, and making sense of lived experiences. The method in which the former is presented creates meaning for the individual as well as the group. Myths are therefore created narratives that a particular group uses to provide context to otherwise incomprehensible realities. Geoffrey Parrinder contends "in the mythologies of every continent there can be distinguished great myths, and others that are of less importance. Some myths dominate and show the character of the religious outlook, while others are less central, repetitive, and fanciful. All kinds of myths need to be taken into account, for altogether they show the values which the society holds dear."[118] These narratives, though composed of both truth and fiction, provide structure to a chaotic and uninformed notion of meaning and purpose in life.

Slaves came to the New World with myths. They possessed within their consciousness stories that provided meaning and explanations for their personal existence, for gods, earth, community, and so on. African myths entailed a belief that symbols, which resulted from myth, also

---

115. Barthes, *Mythologies*, 217.
116. Van Der Leeuw, *Religion in Essence and Manifestation*, 413.
117. Ibid.
118. Parrinder, *African Mythology*, 16.

produce meaning.[119] This sequential understanding of cosmology helps us to appreciate African reverence and respect for the priest. He or she was a representative, a symbol, of God and the ancestors. In Africa, leading priests performed rituals on behalf of the entire community.[120] Priests were required to undergo extensive training in "traditional wisdom, rituals, and practices."[121] Within the scope of their duties, priests would have been responsible also for conveying narratives regarding natural and supernatural things alike. To the African, every celestial and terrestrial phenomenon was of significance. For these realties influenced the balance of the African cosmos; therefore, it was imperative to understand the origin of a phenomenon. Doing so decreased the probability of disrupting the balance of cosmological order. Africans would have come to the New World with their own stories about creation and God.

One African belief illustrates that "God is father and mother of men and animals. He is not often thought of as having been born, since he is eternal, but there is a story that says he was born of a woman with one breast. His wife is spoken of, and the hard brown rings which form the body of a centipede or millipede are called the ivory bracelets of the wife of God."[122] The Dogon people of western Sudan believe that "in the beginning the one God, Amma, created the sun and moon like pots, his first invention. The sun is white hot and surrounded by eight rings of red copper, and the moon is the same shape with rings of white copper. The stars came from pellets of clay that Amma flung into space. To create the earth he squeezed lump of clay, as he had done for the stars, and threw it into space."[123] The Dogon also have a myth about fire. In this story, the first ancestors of man stole fire from the female Nummo; she threw a lightning bolt at him, but to no avail. The male Nummo subsequently threw a lightning bolt, but the ancestor blocked it and escaped to earth by sliding down a rainbow.[124] The Ila people of Zambia believe that God created men and charged them to take care of what he provided to them. But the men saw that they had been blessed with a great harvest, so they ate until they could no longer eat.[125]

119. Parrinder, *Religion in Africa*, 31.
120. Ibid., 76.
121. Ibid., 75.
122. Parrinder, *African Mythology*, 19.
123. Ibid., 24.
124. Ibid., 27.
125. Ibid., 24.

Mythical Meaning of the Slave Preacher

Although African peoples' interpretation of the Supreme God differed based on their locale and traditional ritualistic practices, the element common to all enslaved Africans would have been their ability to construct a sensible reality out of an experience that they did not fully comprehend. These stories, and many others, allowed the slaves to create a rationale and purpose. Everything had meaning—from the great sun to the lowly soil of Africa. It all had purpose.

Once in the Americas, enslaved Africans, therefore, had to construct a context from which to interpret the Christian God. They were not opposed to the idea of a God other than their respective deities. They were simply taken aback by the symbols (such as Christian slave traders) that represented this Christian God's power and authority. Some slaves interpreted the Christian God based on the actions of Christian symbols; but there were slaves who found in Jesus a common experience of oppression. Thus, the *ideal* Jesus became a friend in a time of trouble.

Every story carried meaning, and every carrier of the message was a symbol of authority. Enslaved Africans were dependent upon the symbols (i.e., slave preachers) to provide direction regarding structure in their New World. The subsequent break between priest and African systems of celestial powers left enslaved Africans vulnerable and confused. Therefore, the slave preacher, acting in an abbreviated capacity of priest, utilized new myths that would speak to the urgency of their new crisis. The slave preacher attempted to accomplish this end via the art of deception.

Deception: The King Buzzard and Brer Rabbit Appropriations

Folktales were considered safe and acceptable among many southern whites. Slave owners allowed stories to be told to their children as a means of entertainment. Unlike languages, drums, and religious practices and rituals, folktales were not outlawed; rather, they were embraced as harmless myths about nature and animals.[126] White slave masters were not privy to the didactical element involved in such a craft. Howard Thurman states that "Deception is perhaps the oldest of all the techniques by which the weak have protected themselves against the strong. Through the ages, at all stages of sentient activity, the weak have survived by fooling the strong."[127]

---

126. Brown, "Negro Folk Expression," 320.
127. Thurman, *Jesus and the Disinherited*, 58.

Existential Togetherness

In the myth of The King Buzzard, there are certainly elements of deception at play. After Tad tells of his peculiar and frightful experience with the huge buzzard in the swamp, Cricket is utterly amazed and simply states, "My God!"[128] Tom, with a flare of disapproval, replies, "Dat ain' no buzzard. I hear 'bout dat ole thing 'fore dis.[129] Tom explains to the fireside attendees that Tad's experience mirrors a story that was told "'way back in slavery— 'way back in Af'ica."[130] There was an African chief who collaborated with slave traders by enticing some Africans from his tribe into a trap. The plan was for the chief to lure his people onto the slave ship, and "dem white folks could ketch 'em an' chain 'em."[131] Apparently, the African chief made this a common practice; until one day, the white Slavers decided that it was time to leave the coast and return no more. They decided, therefore, to capture the chief as well. He rejected capture, but to no avail. "So dey knocked dat nigger down an' put chain on him an' brung him to dis country."[132] When he died, heaven rejected him and hell did not desire him. The Great Master, as a result of his treacherous deeds, decided to make the African chief wander the earth for eternity. Moreover, his spirit would manifest as a great buzzard, "an' dat carrion must be he food."[133]

Tad interpreted his experience as being one in which a supernatural beast attempted to devour him. He had indeed encountered a beast, but this beast was not meant to harm him. Rather, his encounter with the buzzard in the swamp was a means by which he must engage notions of communal morality and deception. First, Tad, as well as other attendees, learned that an African chief betrayed his people for money and other European accoutrements. Interestingly enough, by way of deception, the chief himself was also captured and sold. This tragic tale of deception exposes the reality of avarice and communal negation. The chief, prior to his capture, had already become an isolationist. His ancestors would have been aware of his traitorous actions, and therefore deposed him from his designated status of honor among the ancestors upon his demise. The fact that *the Great Master* turned him into a buzzard implies that he was regarded as the scum of the earth.

---

128. Adams, *Nigger to Nigger*, 14.
129. Ibid.
130. Ibid.
131. Ibid.
132. Ibid.
133. Ibid., 15.

Slaves on southern plantations would have shared this story within the community while sitting by a fire or situated in a communal cabin. The moral lesson would have been that slaves who deem it acceptable to betray another slave—in thought and/or deed—were doomed culturally, morally, physically, and spiritually. Whites were not be trusted; additionally, slaves who put their trust in whites were often viewed as traitors. One slave traitor in coastal Georgia, being asked whether Mr. Blue [the overseer] was hard on the slaves, replied:

> No, ma'am, he ain hahd, he jis caahn make um unduhstans. Dey's foolish actin. He got tuh whip um, Mr. Blue, he ain hab no choice. Anyways, he whip um good an dey gits tuhgedduh an stick duh hoe in duh fiel an den say 'quack, quack, quack,' an dey riz up in duh sky an tun hesef intuh buzzuds an fly right back tuh Africa.[134]

The King buzzard myth may have been embraced by traitor slaves as simply a story of entertainment and folklore; following this logic, it seems that some slaves would have used language from the story as a means of employing slave cultural colloquialisms. The astute slaves, however, located themselves in the myth and understood that bodies in chains do not necessarily correlate to understandings of ethical morality. The King Buzzard myth, therefore, inspired the well intentioned slave always to promote communal togetherness, and to be alert to the actions of ill-fated slaves who sought to deceive the community for a better lot in this world.

Brer Rabbit, the trickster-transformer hero,[135] is another myth that resonated with slaves in terms of how they viewed and processed deception in slave culture. Brer Rabbit stories emanate from the Wolof tales that were repeated from the Hausa, Fulani, and Mandinka peoples.[136] Slaves viewed their enslavement as an act of evil, and desired to rid themselves of such an experience. However, they processed their thoughts of freedom within the overwhelming reality of their lack of tangible power. They did not own land, boats, nor themselves. They were considered property. This view, of course, inspired them to use their ingenuity as a weapon of choice. Deception is about survival. Geoffrey Parrinder asserts that the deceptive Brer Rabbit myth has its origins in Africa:

---

134. Johnson, *Drums and Shadows*, 141.
135. Long, *Significations*, 196.
136. Holloway, "The Origins of African-American Culture," 16.

All across Africa fables are told of the cleverness, deceit and triumph of the spider or the hare, called various names according to the language. These yarns were taken to America by the slaves and became the Brer Rabbit tales related by Uncle Remus. There are no rabbits in tropical Africa, and the clever animal is really a hare, which depends on its speed and cunning to protect itself against the dangers of the open Sudan and savannah country. Its chief enemy is the hyena, the Brer Fox of the American versions.[137]

Brer Rabbit was weaker and smaller than most of his foes; yet Brer Rabbit invariably came out of a situation as the victor. Psychologically speaking, stories of the weak defeating the strong provided a sense of hope for the enslaved. In the physical world the slave was limited in defeating the enemy. But stories provided the psychological latitude to envision themselves as creators of their own destinies. In an oppressive situation, where defeat was surely certain, Brer Rabbit always seemed to defy the odds.

> "All right, Brer Wolf, throw me down the well," said Brer Rabbit. "That's an easy way to die, but I'm surely going to smell up your drinking water, sir."
>
> "No, I'm not going to drown you," said Brer Wolf. "Drowning is too good for you." Then Brer Wolf thought and thought and scratched his head and pulled his chin whiskers. Finally he said, "I know what I'm going to do with you. I'll throw you in the briar patch."
>
> "Oh, no, Brer Wolf," cried Brer Rabbit. "Please, sir, don't throw me in the briar patch. Those briars will tear up my hide, pull out my hair, and scratch out my eyes. That'll be an awful way to die, Brer Wolf. Please, sir, don't do that to me."
>
> "That's exactly what I'll do with you," said Brer Wolf all happy-like. Then he caught Brer Rabbit by his hind legs, whirled him around and around over his head, and threw him way over into the middle of the briar patch.
>
> After a minute or two, Brer Rabbit stood up on his hind legs and laughed at Brer Wolf and said to him, "Thank you, Brer Wolf, thank you. This is the place where I was born. My grandmother and grandfather and all my family were born right here in the briar patch."[138]

Don S. McKinney observes that "cunning is the power of the mind whose disciplined use may effect transformation in the balance of physical

---

137. Parrinder, *African Mythology*, 128.
138. Faulkner, *The Days When the Animals Talked*, 127.

power in the world."¹³⁹ Arthur Huff Fauset suggests that the Brer Rabbit character had an antagonistic relationship with a Buzzard in African folklore. The Buzzard, for instance, decided to starve Brer Rabbit to death by sealing him in a hole for five days. Every day the Buzzard would come by the sealed hole an'sing:

> Diddledum-diddledum-day-day. Young man, I'm here. Brer Rabbit he sing it after him. Every day Buzzard would come by singing louder an' louder and every day Brer Rabbit would get "lower an 'lower." De las' day Buzzard sing louder still; but brer Rabbit he very faint. He kin jes' barely say:
>
> Didd—le—dum—didd le—dum
>
> d—a—a—-d—a—a
>
> So Buzzard decide it is time to take Rabbit home to is little ones. As he was carryin' Rabbit to his little ones he said:
>
> Diddledum-diddledum-day-day
>
> Young man, here he.
>
> All come 'round de table. Dey meant to eat him. Had knives an' everything, an' were jes' gonna cut him up when de father said:
>
> Diddledum-diddledum-day-day
>
> Young man, let's eat.
>
> But jes'den ol' Brer Rabbit jumped up from de table an' said:
>
> Diddledum-diddledum-day-day
>
> Young man, I'm gone.
>
> Stepped on a pin
>
> Hit bent
>
> That's the way he went.¹⁴⁰

The mythical exchange between Brer Rabbit and the Buzzard could be an indication that Africans were aware of several instances in which chiefs attempted to trick Africans into situations that would ultimately be the cause of their demise. The Brer Rabbit myths taught slaves how to use mind over might; additionally, they learned that deception and cunning must be employed if survival was to become a primary goal. So too the

---

139. McKinney, "Brer Rabbit," 45.

140. Fauset, "American Negro Folk Literature," 248–49.

slave preacher, as the leader in the community, used the myths to forge an ethos of togetherness and create a space in which they could authentically worship God.

The hush/brush harbors (e.g., hidden paths in thickets, woods, swamps, and forests) was a secret place where slaves would come together to worship. Brush harbor also referred to the dense woods that slaves would have to navigate in order to reach a location they deemed adequate. Slaves would align four heavy forked branches to form a frame, then lay poles across the frame, and place brush on top and along the sides to form a wall. There was one door that was accessed from several beaten paths.[141] It was in this space that the slave preacher preached the gospel. An ex-slave from Mississippi expressed how the slave preacher spoke to his heart in a particular meeting:

> Dey was some mighty good meetins' on de place. Old Daddy Young was 'bout de bes' Preacher us ever had. Dey was plenty o' niggers dere 'cause it was a powerful big place. Old Daddy could sho' make 'em shout an' roll. Us have to hol' some of 'em dey'd git so happy. I knowed I had 'ligion when I got baptized. Dey took me out in de river an' it took two of 'em to put me under. When I come up I tol' 'em, 'turn me loose, I believe I can walk right on top o' de water.' Dey don' hab no 'ligion lak dat now-a-days.[142]

The Art of Preaching

Achieving authority was important in terms of establishing the preacher's credibility within the community. The people had to be sure: just like the neophyte priest was under the tutelage of the prophet priest, it had to be clear that the slave preacher had also been under the divine tutelage of God. There had to be evidence that a slave preacher had indeed been *Struck Dead by God*. For this experience empowered the preacher to preach proficiently on the biblical text. Slaves understood that authentic slave religion should speak to the need of the slave. This entailed a presentation of biblical messages about God's relatedness to the marginalized of the slave community. The typical slave preacher, however, did not possess the tools to grapple hermeneutically with biblical exegesis, as it was illegal for slaves to read

---

141. Rawick, *Georgia Narratives*, 197, in Rawick, *The American Slave*.
142. Rawick, *Mississippi Narratives*, 58, in Rawick, *The American Slave*.

Mythical Meaning of the Slave Preacher

and write throughout the period of slavery. There were instances, however, when black preachers became acquainted with the Bible via white preachers (e.g., Harry "Black Harry" Hoosier and John Jasper). Being in close proximity to educated white preachers afforded slave preachers the opportunity to receive a biblical education via observation. Taking seriously the nature of their responsibility, some slave preachers embraced this indirect method of instruction and appropriated it to align with the religious sensibilities of the slave community. One ex-slave, regarding the lack of formal education of the slave preacher, stated, "he never learned no real readin' and writin' but he sure knowed his Bible and would hold his hand out and make like he was readin' and preach de purtiest preachin' you ever heard."[143] Slave owners often hired slave preachers to preach to their slaves. Understanding the communal influence of the slave preacher, owners used them to reiterate notions of submissiveness and obedience among the masses; although this was done successfully in many instances, an ex-slave remembered when "a yellow man preached to us. She [mistress] had him preach how we was to obey our master and missy if we want to go to heaven, but when she wasn't there, he came out preachin' from the Bible."[144]

The slave preacher's sermons were filled with *vivid imagery*, and delivered in the most dramatic fashion.[145] For the enslaved, sermons were ways in which God spoke to their inner beings. The climax usually entailed an image of expectation. Heaven was a place where all of the slaves' problems were replaced with joy, rest, relaxation, love, and affirmation. In order to make this picture come to life, the slave preacher employed a certain rhythmic cadence that allowed the listeners to journey with him as he spoke words of transcendence:

> Old John the Revelator, aha! A-looking over yonder, aha! In bright glory, aha! "Oh, what do you see, John?" aha! "I see a number, aha! A great number, aha! A host that no man can number, aha! "Who are these, aha!" I heard the angel Gabriel when he answered, aha! "These are they that come up through hard trails and great tribulations, aha! Who washed their robes, aha! and are made them white in the blood of the Lamb, aha! They are now shouting around the throne of God, aha! Well, oh, brothers! Ain't you glad that you have already been in the dressing room, had your everlasting garments fitted on, sandals on your feet? We born of God, aha! are shod for

143. Yetman, *Voices from Slavery*, 335.

144. Ibid., 337.

145. Raboteau, *Slave Religion*, 235.

traveling, aha! Oh, glory to God! It want be long before some of us here, aha! will bid farewell, aha! take the wings of the morning, aha! where there'll be no more sin and sorrow, aha! no more weeping and mourning, aha! We can just walk around, brother, aha! go over and shake hands with old Moses, aha! see Father Abraham, aha! talk with Peter, Matthew, Luke and John, aha! And, oh yes, glory to God! We will want to see our Savior, the Lamb that was slain, ha! They tell me that his face outshines the sun, aha! but we can look on him, aha! because we will be like him. And then, oh brother, oh brother, we will just fly from cherubim to cherubim. There with the angels we will eat off the welcome table, aha! Soon! Soon, we will all be gathered together over yonder. Brothers ain't you glad you done died the sinner-death and don't have to die no more? When we rise to fly that morning, we can fly with healing in our wings. Now, if you don't hear my voice no more, aha! remember, I am a Hebrew child, aha! Just meet me over yonder, aha! on the other side of the River Jordan, away in the third heaven.[146]

The slave preacher envisioned preaching as a dialogue, and so in a sense handed the sermon over to the congregation. This simply means that the preacher did not possess primary ownership of the material. The sermon was treated as God's words, for God's people. Also, the slave sermon had a call and response element to it. This not only involved the people, but alerted the preacher to any moments of irrelevancy. The sermon was very much relevant to the preacher, but it had very little relevance if the people could not become emotionally attached to its meaning. The slave preacher wanted to feel the emotional tension of the congregation; in turn, the congregation wanted to feel the intensity of the preacher. This rhetorical tension produced an experience in which both preacher and people expected a response to their respective emotional pleas. Moreover, when climax was achieved, a euphoric demonstration was in view for all to see and hear. One slave preacher in New Orleans was constantly confirmed by slaves' interrupting cries of affirmation: 'Yes, glory!' 'that's it, hit him again! Hit him again! Oh, glory! hi! hi glory!' 'glory, glory, glory,!' 'Glory!-oh, yes! Yes!—sweet Lord! Sweet Lord! 'yes, sir! Oh, Lord yes!' 'yes! Yes!' 'oh! Lord! Help us!' 'Ha! Ha! Ha!' 'Glory to the Lord!'[147]

The slave preacher also used parallelism to rhetorical effect. He mentioned slavery in Egypt as a means of correlating Hebrew bondage with that

---

146. Johnson, *God Struck Me Dead*, 8.
147. Olmstead, *A Journey in the Back Country*, 187–96.

of African American bondage. The central motif in such a parallel is the notion that God is the myth and Moses is the symbol. Moses spoke to the people on behalf of God. Moses also spoke to God on behalf of the people, and challenged the temporal power structures that stood as a gulf between God and the enslaved. The slave preacher, on behalf of the enslaved, demanded freedom from bondage as a means to worship God more authentically. To be sure, the slaves' hush harbor experiences were indeed genuine; however, they had to worship in secret. The slave preacher certainly would have used the following spirituals when communicating the parallels of biblical narratives and slave narrative:

> Didn't my Lord deliver Daniel,
> Deliver Daniel,
> Deliver Daniel,
> Didn't my Lord deliver Daniel,
> And why not every man.
>
> He delivered Daniel from the lion's den,
> Jonah from the belly of the whale,
> And the Hebrew Children from the fiery furnace,
> And why not every man.[148]

and

> When Israel was in Egypt's Land,
> Let my people go.
> Go down, Moses, way down in Egypt's Land,
> Tell Old Pharaoh, let my people go.[149]

The slave preacher also used singing as a means of expanding the sermonic experience. John Jasper, the great funeral preacher, would use an old *Dr. Watts hymn* to extend the emotional climax of a sermon. Slaves understood a *Dr. Watts* to be an invitation to join the preacher in a back-and-forth rhythmic pattern of singing exchanges. This experience afforded the opportunity for every slave present to become emotionally engaged in the worship experience. This elevated mode of collaborative musical communication can be traced to the African use of the drum. The seventeenth

---

148. Cone, *The Spirituals and the Blues*, 35.
149. Courlander, *Negro Folk Music*, 42.

and eighteenth-century slave embraced religious worship with an understanding that drums would be used to authenticate the religious experience. Ex-slave Wallace told a WPA interviewer that "we sho did hab big time goin tuh chuch in doze days. Not many uh deze Nigguhs kin shout tuhday duh way us could den. Yuh needs a drum fuh shoutin."[150] Drums were also used to alert slaves to meetings as well as funerals, which both always included singing, chanting, praying, and clapping. As a means of deterring communal gathering of slaves, Virginia outlawed the use of drums in 1680.[151] Nevertheless, generation after generation of slaves continued to sing. They sang of heaven being a sanctuary of freedom from the harsh reality of enslavement:

> "Jordan River, I'm bound to go'
> Bound to go, bound to go, —
> Jordan River, I'm bound to go,
> And bid 'em fare ye well.[152]

And:
> "Dere's no rain to wet you,
> O, yes, I want to go home.
> Dere's no sun to burn you,
> O, yes, I want to go home;
> O, push along, believers,
> O, yes.[153]

The slaves also sang about freedom and togetherness.

> When we all meet in heaven,
> there is no parting there;
> when we all meet in heaven,
> there is no parting there.[154]

Early scholarly writing on the slave preacher includes analyses on interactions and engagements with the community. Scholars contend that the slave preacher engaged the community and the outside world via

150. Johnson, *Drums and Shadows*, 140.
151. Guild, *Black Laws of Virginia*, 45–46.
152. Higginson, "Slave Songs and Spirituals," 114.
153. Ibid., 117.
154. Stroyer, *My Life in the South*, 41.

Mythical Meaning of the Slave Preacher

manipulation, intellectualism, radicalism, and elitism. The reality of the existential crisis also thrust the slave preacher into a realm that caused him to become a deceiver in the interests of survival, to maneuver in a world in which danger was omnipresent. The slave preacher also led his community through the many storms of slave life (e.g., rapes, familial separations, lynchings, floggings, beatings, and so on). At every stage of religious, social, and political transition, the slave preacher was there operating as a prophet of God, explaining the cosmological happenings of the here-and-now moment. Nat Turner, the infamous Baptist slave preacher, interpreted the religious, social, and political climate to indicate a shift in a meaningful trajectory for the enslaved. Operating in the old spirit of the slave preacher, Nat Turner reasoned that violence could secure a more expedient response to slaves' desire for abolition; rather than preach a here-after message of accommodation, Turner believed that violent direct action could secure liberation in a space that slaves helped build in the here and now. Turner's radical notion of liberation had meager success. His thirst for revenge was quenched as he and his companions journeyed from plantation to plantation—killing white children, men, and women (fifty-five in all). Betrayed by a slave boy in his party, the rebellion was quashed and the participants were punished accordingly. As a result of Turner's violent protest, the white social structure condemned and outlawed slave preaching.

Although instances exist in which some slave preachers were allowed to practice subsequently, the overwhelming response was to deny such a privilege to any slave, and although the invisible institution was a viable place to continue in the tradition of the forebears, the slave preacher used unique ways to deceive the foe (i.e., the slave master) who was earnestly seeking to locate slave deceptions. Willis Williams, a slave preacher from Georgia, would have had to deal with the social stigma of being in such a role. His son, A. D. Williams, would also become a preacher and pastor in Atlanta, Georgia; and his great-grandson, Martin Luther King Jr. would do the opposite of Turner by adopting a nonviolent direct action approach as a means of uplifting black people to a better dimension in society. As a recipient of the slave preacher tradition, King would continue to illume the theme of togetherness throughout his prophetic tenure.

EXCURSUS

Du Bois, Racism, and Black Religion

W. E. B. Du Bois is a prominent figure within the field of African American religious studies. His groundbreaking study of *The Negro Church* (1903) unpacked the complex nature of what it means to be both religious and black in America. Such meaning, for Du Bois, was ultimately interpreted through the leadership role of the preacher. As was the case in Africa, as well as the African American experience of slavery, the black religious leader was responsible for interpreting the movement of the divine within the cultural realm of black people(s). Prior to Dr. Martin Luther King's ascension to the par excellence role as black religious leader of the civil rights movement, Du Bois, for half a century, promoted the notion that the pursuit of truth must be the primary goal of black people. Theirs [African Americans] was a history filled with ingenuity and significance. White religion promoted the idea that blacks were culturally ignorant of God prior to, and during, their enslavement. Black religion, on the other hand, presented the unapologetic truth that blacks were historically aware of their religious significance and cultural worth. Nevertheless, the process of slavery distorted truth and left gaps of doubt within the African American psyche. The Duboisian task of black religion, then, is to unearth historical fact of African religious ingenuity—thereby establishing a foundational truth from which oppressed blacks could obtain enough confidence to gain their rightful place within American society. This section will illume Du Bois' journey as a young privileged New Englander whose notion of blackness would be expanded by personal engagements with regional racism, education, and cultural religion. Dr. King, a descendant of the slave preaching tradition, would continue to combat racist ideology through Duboisian methods of truth seeking, and lead blacks to their proper place in God's world.

EXCURSUS

As a young boy growing up in Great Barrington, Massachusetts, Du Bois was aware of his racial distinction. There were but a few black families in the town, and the Du Bois family visited an A.M.E church periodically. Although afforded the privilege of education, the formal structure of Du Bois' schooling did not leave much room for personal reflection about the essence of the African American experience. Du Bois was certainly aware that being African American placed him in a disenfranchised category, which he would later conclude to be based on ignorant concepts of race inferiority. As he so poignantly stated, "I realized that some folks, a few, even several, actually considered my brown skin a misfortune."[1] When he informed people that he desired to attend Harvard, he recollects, "my white friends hesitated and my colored friends were silent."[2] The experience of being torn between black and white realities, what he would later term *Double Consciousness*, was perhaps first illumined during this same period. He would define such an experience in *The Souls of Black Folk* with acumen as a learned PhD from Harvard.

In the instance with his friends, both black and white, he sees a fundamental theme of inferiority being posited by both sides. Du Bois' white friends feel that he is not good enough and his black friends are taken aback by the very presumption that he has equality with symbols of white power and privilege. Neither side believes that Du Bois is capable of achieving his goal. Their lack of confidence is not based on evidence of any intellectual disabilities; rather, their conclusion is based on a premise that situates the color of Du Bois' skin as a predestined condition of nothingness. He would eventually attend and graduate Fisk University before attending Harvard and the University of Berlin. Interestingly enough, Du Bois was offered a scholarship to attend Hartford Theological Seminary.[3]

Du Bois considered the days of his early life to be that of disillusion. He concluded that what he deemed to be "Will and Ability was sheer luck!"[4] Du Bois realized that his place in the world was chance as there were so many other talented black people without his access to privilege and influence. This is not to suggest that Du Bois lacked confidence in his intellectual gifts and abilities; he simply had a dialectical personality that was neither completely arrogant nor humble. He found solace in a realm between the

---

1. Du Bois, *Dark Water*, 6.
2. Ibid., 7.
3. Marable, *W. E. B. Du Bois*, 11.
4. Du Bois, *Dark Water*, 9.

two. But there he stood in the presence of the mighty *zeitgeist*, a man with an uncanny ability to articulate to the world the yearnings of millions of oppressed souls. A sense of cultural responsibility may have been a central thrust of Du Bois' dogged pursuit to create more space and opportunity for marginalized African Americans. But Du Bois would soon come to realize that racist ideology does not acquiesce based on historical critiques from an Ivy League, educated black. Despite his academic pedigree, Du Bois experienced racism at all levels. White power existed at the lowest sphere in life, as well as the highest. The normative thought in the early twentieth century was that African Americans were descendants of uncivilized people; even if some were as gifted as a W. E. B. Du Bois, such a one nevertheless received a question mark because of his *abnormal* heritage. Curtis Evans argues that a study on the topic of black life, in Du Bois' day, was viewed as nothing more than an attempt to research what had already been established via biased scholarship.[5] This issue constantly confronted Du Bois. In a sense, he was fighting an intellectual war on two fronts. On one hand, he had to obtain accurate truth through scientific study in order to refute scholarly patterns of racist ideology; on the other, Du Bois had to inspire a downtrodden people to learn about their past as a means of sustaining themselves in the present and progressing toward the future. Du Bois was the first scholar, as Werner Lange contends, to present an ethnography of Afro-American life (1894–1915), but racial discrimination within the academy hindered such distinguished recognition and contribution.[6] The study of black existence was a waste of time as some scholars believed the early presuppositions about blackness solidified their position in history as inferior being. Nevertheless, Du Bois, being the pragmatic researcher that he was, used scientific inquiry to dismantle illogical notions regarding blackness.[7]

Du Bois was also the first scholar, black or white, to conduct a scientific study on the African American religious experience.[8] Although he refrained from overextending the notion that the Negro Church was an ontological representation of black life, Du Bois nevertheless understood the *Black Church* to be a creative space in which collectively oppressed black folk sought opportunity to function as liberated human beings. In this sacred location, blacks were free to engage authentically in religious worship,

---

5. Evans, "W. E. B. Du Bois," 270.
6. Lange, "W. E. B. Du Bois and the First Scientific Study of Afro-America," 2.
7. Gordon, "Du Bois's Humanistic Philosophy of Human Sciences," 265–80.
8. See Du Bois, *The Negro Church*.

receive moral guidance, participate in communal/political conversation, take advantage of limited educational opportunities, as well as engage in trivial pursuits such as communal gossip and so on. This culturally concentrated space, for Du Bois, was a place of diversified cathartic expression. But more than that, the Black Church became a conduit through which enslaved African Americans gathered to voice their sorrow. Slave religion, Du Bois reasoned, was a created space in which enslaved African Americans sought respite from the all-consuming reality of slavery. In this space, the suppressed voices of the enslaved were finally released through bodily movement and vocal shrieking. With experience in the south, acquisition of a quality education, and an extensive independent study in African American history, Du Bois would come to believe of enslaved Africans that

> Nothing suited his condition better than the doctrines of passive submission embodied in the newly learned Christianity. Slave masters early realized this, and cheerfully aided religious propaganda within certain bounds. The long system of repression and degradation of the Negro tended to emphasize the elements in his character which made him a valuable chattel: courtesy became humility, moral strength degenerated into submission, and the exquisite native appreciation of the beautiful became an infinite capacity for dumb suffering. The Negro, losing the joy of this world, eagerly seized upon the offered conceptions of the next; the avenging spirit of the Lord enjoining patience in this world, under sorrow and tribulation until the Great Day when He should lead His dark children home,—this became his comforting dream. His preacher repeated the prophecy, and his bards sang,— "Children, we all shall be free, When the Lord shall appear."

Du Bois concluded that the Europeans' strategy was to supplant dominance across the globe. Religion was a tactic used to establish righteous claim to this divine right. Although he brilliantly analyzed the system that was used to enslave Africans, he nevertheless understood that the tactic employed within the system was very effective; thus, his fervent desire for the training of the black mind was of the utmost concern. Additionally, Du Bois' thought regarding the employment of the Talented Tenth philosophy was in no way an attempt to position himself above the worth of any African American, nor was it a claim that ninety percent of the masses have nothing of worth to contribute. Du Bois embraced the Talented Tenth philosophy in the early stages of his career; pragmatically speaking, the majority of African American had limited worth as they were not afforded the opportunity to learn their rich history. Du Bois concluded that the *talented* ten percent, people who have received higher education and are enlightened regarding the plight of black America, are obligated to do more in terms of scholarship and establishing leadership roles, to aid in debunking false narratives about the African American experience.

In 1948 Du Bois delivered an address to the Grand Boulé.[9] Before this vast array of black intelligentsia, he revealed a new method of progress. He advocated for "the concept of group-leadership, not simply educated and self-sacrificing, but with clear vision of present world conditions and dangers, and conducting American Negroes to alliance with culture groups in Europe, America, Asia and Africa, and looking toward a new world culture. We can do it. We have the ability. The question is, have we the will?"[10] The *willing spirit* to which Du Bois refers is the existential responsibility of every individual to locate within their own lived experience a truth worth fighting for. Du Bois understood that the vast majority of African Americans were detached from notions of historical imagination. The task, then, for Du Bois was to advocate for a one hundred year[11] educational revival, which would enlighten the masses, thereby creating a context from which inspiration could translate into a motivational drive for the uplift of self and the black race. Education, however, was more than a structured format of, and retention of information. African Americans, according to Du Bois, had to learn how to think critically regarding their most peculiar existence. While a student at Fisk University, Du Bois learned that his structured college education did not provide a historical lesson in the lived experience of African Americans. Thanks to his curious and critical mind, Du Bois' early collegiate experience was therefore supplemented with an ad hoc field education.

The young Du Bois ventured out into the Tennessee countryside one summer and encountered, deep within the woods, a phenomenon that would place him in direct contact with another dimension of black religious worship. As Manning Marable notes, "Such deep expressions of spirituality were utterly new to him."[12] It was something mysterious, as Du

---

9. Founded in 1900, Henry McKee Minton and a small group of his colleagues founded Sigma Pi Phi Fraternity, the nation's first black Greek-letter Fraternity, as a means of fostering social support for black professionals.

10. Gates and West, *The Future of the Race*, 168.

11. Du Bois, "Dusk of Dawn," 600.

12. Marable, *W. E. B. Du Bois*, 10.

Bois viewed it, about the "rhythmic cadence of song—soft, thrilling, powerful, that swelled and died sorrowfully in our ears."[13] The extended moans of alto, soprano, and tenor engulfed the consciousness of Du Bois, and like the Hebrew Prophet Ezekiel, he *sat where they sat*. He became mesmerized in what Sterling Stuckey refers to as the position of participant-observer. Although Du Bois had been exposed to both black and white New England religious experiences, no previous religious encounter had prepared him for such an emotional and physical expression of faith. I do not suspect that Du Bois was racially conflicted by such an experience as some scholars suggest; rather, I believe that he was prompted to consider 1) how this experience differed so drastically from that of New England rigid standards, and 2) how this experience existentially resonated with a component of his psyche that had been unaffected until that very moment of engagement. Although New England in the late nineteenth/early twentieth century was more covert in its dealings with race relations than states located in the Deep South, Du Bois, at the age of thirteen, nevertheless was aware and subject to acts of racial intolerance.[14]

> Already in my boyhood this matter of color loomed significantly. My skin was darker than that of my schoolmates. My family confined itself not entirely but largely to people of this same darker hue. Even when in fact the color was lighter, this was an unimportant variation from the norm. As I grew older, and saw the peoples of the land and of the world, the problem changed from a simple thing of color, to a broader, deeper matter of social condition: to millions of folk born of dark slaves, with the slave heritage in mind and home; millions of people spawned in compulsory ignorance; to a whole problem of the uplift of the lowly who formed the darker races. This social condition pictured itself gradually in my mind as a matter of education, as a matter of knowledge; as a matter of scientific procedure in a world which had become scientific in concept. Later, however, all this frame of concept became blurred and distorted. There was evidently evil and hindrance blocking the way of life. Not science alone could settle this matter, but force must come to its aid. The black world must fight for freedom. It must fight with the weapons of Truth, with the sword of the intrepid, uncompromising Spirit, with organization in boycott, propaganda and mob frenzy.[15]

13. Du Bois, *Souls of Black Folk*, 134.
14. Lewis, *W. E. B. Du Bois*, 34.
15. Du Bois, "Dusk of Dawn," 556–57.

The formal study of Africa and the different movements of the African American slave experience occurred during Du Bois' post Fisk days. Prior to the Great Debate between Herskovits and Frazier,[16] Du Bois had located an African retention within his own family heritage. The song that his grandfather's grandmother brought over from Africa was still being sung to children two hundred years later. Du Bois asserted that the slave songs that he heard in the south were also the songs that he heard growing up in New England. "They came out of the South unknown to me," he admits, "one by one, and yet at once I knew them as of me and of mine."[17] Although the Du Bois' were members of a white religious community, the communal aspect of black life and culture exposed W. E. B. to a bond that grafted him into a cultural experience that crossed geography and region. However, one must note "that the basis of his moral fervor," as Arnold Rampersad contends, "was the iron of Puritan ethics, initially instilled in him in the First Congregational Church of Great Barrington."[18] This zeal of snobbishness must be what Rampersad had in mind when he concluded that Du Bois had become an "apostle of elitism and a political conservative"[19] after his return from his studies at the University of Berlin. Du Bois would argue, however, that the use of European accoutrements need not imply a contradiction in race loyalty.

Du Bois was a man of sound religious convictions. In fact, the beginning portion of his *Credo* reads: "I believe in God, who made of one blood all nations that on earth do dwell. I believe that all men, black and brown and white, are brothers, varying through time and opportunity, in form and

---

16. The Herskovits and Frazier *Great Debate* focused on two theses:
Herskovits' cultural retention thesis, which argued for the continuity of West African carryovers in African American religion and culture. Herskovits alluded to spirit possession (West African sense of intimacy with Deity). Dancing with African steps and identical motor behavior. Singing that derives in manner, if not actual form, directly from Africa (the polyrhythmic character of music and its relation to dance).
Frazier's cultural annihilation thesis, which posited that the experience of slavery and minority status in Anglo-Saxon culture had led to the annihilation of African culture in the U.S.—with one exception (Gullah) and that African culture, was replaced with a Jim Crow imitation of religion, mores, and values of white society. So Frazier took on an assimilationist viewpoint. The assimilationist model embraces the view that black people in the U.S. are completely American culturally, and that their religion should be studied merely as a variety of American religion.

17. Du Bois, *Souls of Black Folk*, 177.

18. Rampersad, *The Art and Imagination of W. E. B. Du Bois*, 5.

19. Ibid., 63.

gift and feature, but differing in no essential particular, and alike in soul and the possibility of infinite development."[20] It seems that Du Bois' notion of European religious truth was replaced along the way with a religiously inquisitive skepticism. This historical pivot led him to a path that would define his academic work for decades to come. Along this trek, according to Lewis V. Baldwin, Du Bois would become the first scholar "to actually utilize and make significant references to the folksongs and their meaning in terms of Black life and culture."[21] Although Du Bois was familiar with religion and the God concept, this encounter with southern black culture and religion set ablaze in him a desire to better understand black cultural dynamics, which gave birth to such an experience as being an African American. David Levering Lewis contends that Du Bois, although exposed to a variety of religious experiences early in life, had not placed much faith in the whole of the Christian canon. If this is true, Du Bois certainly displayed remarkable use of Christian theology in prayers that he wrote for his students at Atlanta University.[22] Regarding humility, Du Bois proposed that they ought to go "back to the lowly barn-yard and the homely cradle of yellow and despised Jew, whom the world has not yet learned to call wonderful, Counsellor, the Mighty God, the Everlasting Father, and the Prince of Peace. Amen."[23] Within this context, Du Bois locates Jesus as the example for leading a life of power and honor, and reminds his audience that community plays a part in individual success. It seems to me that Du Bois understood the concept of religion to encompass more than just spiritual significations; he applies the concept of religion to that of everyday activity, thinking, and being. On another occasion, he pleads, "Let us remember, O God, that our religion in life is expressed in our work, and therefore in this school it is shown in the way we conquer our studies—not entirely in our marks but in the honesty of our endeavor, the thoroughness of our accomplishment and the singleness and purity of our purpose."[24] Du Bois even declares "wave on wave, each with increasing virulence, is dashing this new religion of whiteness on the shores of our time."[25] For Du

20. Du Bois, *Dark Water*, 1.

21. Baldwin, *Culture as an Aspect of Black History*, 6.

22. These prayers were presented between the academic years of 1909 and 1910. See Du Bois, *Prayers for Dark People*, 3–75.

23. Du Bois, *Prayers for Dark People*, 15.

24. Ibid, 33.

25. Du Bois, "The Souls of White Folk," 923–38.

Bois, religion entails the historical and cultural movements of life. Much like African cosmology, Du Bois understands black religion to have a communal focus. This was evident in his study of *The Negro Church*. The early twentieth-century Black Church was indeed the "social centre of Negro life in the United States."[26] Every possible societal need was addressed within the black religious community because that is where communal resources were gathered and distributed. The order of the social movement within this small cultural sphere of existence was established and maintained by the preacher; thus indirectly positioning the black preacher as the moral authority regarding communal existence.

Du Bois's mentor and professor, William James, understood life and religious experience to be interconnected. The stronger willed, he asserted, should strengthen the weaker willed as they both co-exist in a reality of mutuality in which progression is dependent upon both elements working together as a unit.[27] James was the first social scientist to apply pragmatic method to the study of religion. The thrust of James's pragmatic method essentially focuses on getting at the essence of a matter, which is defined as truth. Getting at the heart of any matter is invariably challenging. Therefore, says James, "The pragmatist clings to facts and concreteness, observes truth at its work in particular cases, and generalizes."[28] Robert Michael Franklin observes the *dialectical tension*[29] in both James's and Du Bois's writings. No doubt when James read a copy of Du Bois's *The Souls of Black Folk*, he would have identified correlations of his pragmatic thinking in Du Bois's analysis of the African American religious experience. I consider *The Souls of Black Folk* to be a seminal religious studies text, for several of its essays pragmatically unveil truth through the prism of African American faith experiences and religious strivings. *Of The Faith of our Fathers, Of Our Spiritual Strivings*, and *The Sorrow Songs* are essays about what is means to be Christian and African American in the early twentieth century America. Du Bois would describe such a reality as "A people thus handicapped ought not be asked to race with the world, but rather allowed to give all its time and thought to its social problems."[30] Du Bois often conflates religious meaning with cultural and societal concerns. *The Souls of Black Folk* follows this

26. Du Bois, *Souls of Black Folk*, 137.
27. James, *The Varieties of Religious Experience*, 136.
28. James, *Pragmatism*, 33.
29. Franklin, *Liberating Visions*, 45.
30. Du Bois, *Souls of Black Folk*, 13.

trajectory. "The Nation has not yet found peace from its sins; the freedman has not yet found in freedom his promised land."[31] This movement is in the tradition of the slave preacher. Du Bois certainly writes with the mind of a scholar and the heart of a prophet; unfortunately, minds grow weary and hearts tend to break.

Du Bois tirelessly worked toward the betterment of the black race; but after enduring government harassment and being denied opportunities to speak and publish work, Du Bois decided to leave the United States and relocate to Ghana. He informed a friend that "we leave for Ghana October 5th and I set no date for return . . . Chin up, and fight on, but realize that American Negroes can't win."[32] In typical manner, Du Bois' dialectical mind encourages an engagement that he believes is unachievable. His pessimism could be attributed to disappointment in black leadership, the white power structure, and/or God. Regardless, Du Bois returned to the land that he heard songs about some eighty years earlier. Africa was his final resting place, because America did not love his body nor respect his brilliance. Du Bois died on August 27, 1963; the next day, Dr. Martin Luther King Jr. would stand before the nation and world and imagine a nation that embraces the truth about its past as a means of living out the ideals of its restorative potentiality. Dr. King, out of admiration and respect for the intellectual giant, also rendered words of praise for the man. In a sense, Du Bois passed the proverbial leadership mantle to Dr. King with both hope and despair. He knew what type of difficulties lay before the African American people, and I believe he knew what would happen to its leader.

The death of Du Bois and the emergence of King as the leader of the civil rights movement coincided with a metaphorical transference of black leadership power. It is reminiscent of the Elijah and Elisha Hebrew narrative in which the aged, and battle weary, prophet transfers power to a younger and more hopeful and spirited prophet. To be sure, by 1963 Dr. King was considered the leader of the civil rights movement. In fact, as early as 1957 King had gained such notoriety that he was featured in *Time Magazine*. Du Bois' indictment in 1951 as a communist spy took attention away from the social injustices that he sought to eradicate using scientific truth. In 1963, Du Bois, no longer a citizen of the United States of America, officially become a citizen of Ghana. White America viewed Du Bois as a

---

31. Ibid., 11.

32. Quoted from West, *The American Evasion of Philosophy*, 149 and Horne, *Black and Red*, 345.

nuisance, a provocateur, and agitator of the status quo. They thought his renunciation of US citizenship would be beneficial because he would finally be out of sight and mind. "But he was an exile, according to King, "only to the land of his birth. He died at home in Africa among his cherished ancestors and he was ignored by pathetically ignorant America but not history."[33]

---

33. King, "Honoring Dr. Du Bois," 114.

4

Martin Luther King Jr. and the Rhetoric of Existential Togetherness

And we walked together for 381 days. That's what we got to learn in the North: Negroes have to learn to stick together. We stuck together. We sent out the call and no Negro rode the buses. It was one of the most amazing things I've seen in my life. And the people of Montgomery asked me to serve as the spokesman, and as president of the new organization—the Montgomery Improvement Association that came into being to lead the boycott—I couldn't say no. And then we started our struggle together.[1]

Dr. Martin Luther King Jr. understood religion, black religion in particular, to be a driving and sustaining force in moments of existential angst. From early childhood, Dr. King was exposed to the survival testimonies of former slaves. Being a descendant of the slave preaching tradition, he understood that the preacher contributed to the construction of such testimonies. For it was the slaver preacher, according to King, who instilled a sense of worth and value in the hearts and minds of the enslaved. This Sunday communal experience was much more than mere religious worship; rather it was a time in which slaves sought enough strength to survive the ordeals awaiting them the remaining days of the week.[2] In a sense, Dr. King saw himself standing in this same privileged tradition.[3]

---

1. King, "Why Jesus Called a Man a Fool," paragraph 31; lines 5–8.
2. King, *Papers*, 6:316.
3 Baldwin, *There is a Balm in Gilead*, 302.

Existential Togetherness

It is not surprising, therefore, that the rhetoric of existential togetherness flows throughout his many sermons, speeches, and writings. In particular, *I've Been to the Mountaintop* is perhaps King's most poignant articulation of existential togetherness praxis within the black community. It is important to note that *I've Been to the Mountaintop*, which was rendered the night prior to his death, also locates the black preacher as the leading force in uniting the black community. Dr. King warned black America that survival and progression of the race was contingent upon individuals learning to work together for the common cause of social and economic equality. In order to progressively live together as brothers and sisters, blacks, according to King, had to first learn how to fight and struggle together. Such an opportunity would present itself in the Deep South.

In 1955, Dr. King was chosen to lead efforts to organize the black masses and improve their social plight of oppression in Montgomery, Alabama. Dr. King's first senior pastorate, Dexter Avenue Baptist Church, is still located just a short distance from the audaciously white state capitol building. The very ordinances and laws that King would come to challenge were debated and legalized just yards away from where he and his parishioners gathered as a community, worshiped God, and discussed political matters. King was unaware, however, that the movement in Montgomery would propel him to an iconic position of a Moses/Jesus like-figure (i.e., someone who is constantly being cosmically lured into a state of divine compliance). King (as well as Du Bois) would often describe such an experience as being captured by the *zeitgeist*.[4] Such an existence is quite burdensome; in Dr. King's case, it was burdensome to the point of being murdered—shot down while engaged in friendly banter on the balcony of The Lorraine Hotel in Memphis, Tennessee.

A former student of Dr. J.T. Francisco, the Chief Examiner who performed Dr. King's autopsy, stated that Dr. Francisco showed King's autopsy pictures to The University of Tennessee medical students. Due to the graphic nature of the images, university officials requested that he cease using such pedagogical tactics in his lectures. He left the university soon thereafter. While viewing the slides, some students would experience nausea due to the gruesome nature of the images. Dr. Francisco wanted them to see, and feel, the sickness of America.[5]

---

4. Smith, *Search for the Beloved Community*, 117 and Lewis, *W. E. B. Du Bois*, 344.
5. John Major, M.D. in discussion with author. January 2018.

King's death is just as important as his life. They both speak to us in our racially intensified state of domestic affairs. The only thing that has changed since the death of King is the tone of America—racism has not been as loud as it had once been (i.e., frequent cross burnings, undisputed lynchings, rapes, and so on), but the volume is currently at a high pitch, and ripe to regress back to its former *loudness*.

King, Symbolism, and Black Heroic Heritage

Martin Luther King, Jr. was a person carved and molded to fit a particular period in history. His giftedness, compassion, faith, devotion, and love were qualities transmitted to him through socially conscious forebears (i.e., men and women who had a cultural connection to a *black messiah*). Jewish notions of *messiah* entail a central belief that such a person is somehow entangled in the fabric of human history. In other words, God unveils such a one at the proper moment in history in order to render aid in fulfilling God's divine prerogatives. Messianic unveilings are not based on personal volition; rather, God selects the proper moment in history to unveil God's intention through a human symbol. Martin Luther King Jr. was such a person.

In 1961 Mike Wallace interviewed Dr. King, and toward the end of that discussion, Wallace asked, "What happens to a man when he becomes owned by a cause? What happens to you as you become the symbol of the segregation struggle? As a man?"[6] King responded by enumerating both the advantages and disadvantages of such a position. When one embraces the reality that people view symbols as somewhat heroic figures, according to King, one must then engage in self-analysis and determine where one stands in light of symbolic comparisons. Such analytical work improves the probability that one's life, both public and private, "serves at least to inspire the individual to seek to rise from the is-ness of his present nature to the eternal ought-ness that forever confronts him."[7] In other words, King believed that the symbolic critique of his life actually compelled him to engage life as a morally maturing individual. The disadvantage associated with a symbolic critique is seen in the lack of privacy afforded to King and his family. King understood his role as a preacher to entail the experience of daily sacrifice. Close readings of heroic symbols such as Moses, Amos,

6. King, *Papers*, 7:164.
7. Ibid.

Existential Togetherness

Jeremiah, Isaiah, and Jesus provided examples of the cost of being the *prophetic voice of God*. Based on King's understanding of the former moral bents, he invariably resolved that prophets should "speak truth to power" and "critique and ultimately eliminate evil and unjust structures, laws and institutions."[8] The black condition, as King understood it, could not be addressed by part-time leaders. The dilemma of blacks in America was one of ignorance and disadvantage. In order to remedy these moral and social ills, King determined that being absent from his personal family life could enhance the probability of all black families gaining better educational / social advantages in the future, as a result of the sacrifice that he was willing to make. The black struggle would require his total dedication. By default, personal dreams and obligations often came second to King's work as a pastor and civil rights leader. He fully understood that the fight for equal justice would be long and hard, but he was willing to commit his whole being to such an effort. King had become possessed by the *zeitgeist*, and soon discovered that "when people get caught up with that which is right and they are willing to sacrifice for it, there is no stopping point short of victory."[9]

Much like his enslaved forebears, King used biblical parallelisms as a means of relating significance and truth to the African American experience. In a sense, King's description of black struggle coincided with the oppressed Hebrews and their struggle to become liberated.

> King often used the traditional biblical language of the Exodus story to describe the struggle of black people to be free. The towering figure of Moses as leader, Egypt as the condition of oppression, Pharaoh as oppressor, the Red Sea as an obstacle to freedom, the wilderness as the transition period between slavery and freedom, and the Promised Land as freedom are all paradigms for those who were themselves engaged in a similar struggle. The Exodus drama was tailor-made for those like King who believed that God was not just involved in the historical; God was actually directing the events of history.[10]

Blacks endowed King with god-like qualities because he exuded the essence of what he believed to be Jesus' highest teaching principle: agape

---

8. Baldwin, *The Voice of Conscience*, 248.
9. King, "I've Been to the Mountain Top," 268.
10. Whatley, *Roots of Resistance*, 25.

love. Jesus' unconditional love for humanity was the ultimate cause of his demise; in this relation, King shared Jesus' fate, and people love him for it.

> When a reporter in Montgomery observed a group cheering King, he observed, "They think he's a Messiah." As King left a courtroom, followers shouted, "Behold the King!" Soon afterward he was introduced as someone who had been "nailed to the cross" for their sake. Several years later, in a ceremony honoring his work, another speaker likened him to Jesus.[11]

This heroic image became all the more pronounced as a result of King's constant reiteration of the Exodus theme of deliverance. King understood, as Herbert Marbury attests, that Egyptian death at the Red Sea symbolizes the death of racism and segregation, but it is only a death that could occur at the hands of the divine.[12] To this extent, God's movement in history was displayed via the acts of Moses. The parting of the Red Sea, for instance, is a narrative that illustrates God and humanity working together to accomplish a certain end, that end being ultimate freedom for the Hebrews. Through such an engagement, the Hebrews crossed over and the Egyptians died in the Red Sea. The manner in which the Hebrew slaves processed reality, however, did not drown in the Red Sea. Moses would have to learn to lead a people who had once been conditioned to think of themselves in terms of personal unworthiness. They were physically free, but the Hebrews would have to become mentally reconditioned in order to live as fully free human beings.

In this sense, Africans Americans became co-creators with God. Before there could be a movement against injustice, some blacks had to learn that their condition in life was unjust. King understood that the black psyche had been damaged by the experience of enslavement. He therefore often referred to a historical context of oppression when giving sermons and speeches. Oppressed African Americans had to accept the fact that they were people of worth, and that God found them to be too worthy to suffer in their current state of existence. God was willing to help, but African Americans had to be willing to embrace freedom by working alongside God. Blacks, therefore, had to become organized as one collective voice—this seems to be one of King's toughest struggles. Ironically, Roy Wilkins, executive director of the National Association for the Advancement of Colored People, was not a supporter of King's *agenda*. King, nevertheless,

---

11. Miller, *Voice of Deliverance*, 173.
12. Marbury, *Pillars of Cloud and Fire*, 154–55.

continued to urge unity and togetherness for the whole of black America. King's symbolic recognition of God's involvement with African Americans was based on God's organized and pragmatic approaches to ultimate liberation. For King, God was a God of reason, order, and structure. It was unreasonable, therefore, to use any method of protest that would run counter to God's agenda for black liberation.

For King, unity did not mean uniformity.[13] African Americans needed to become unified in their approach toward freedom. The proper means to achieve freedom was often debated among black leaders; nevertheless, the common struggle for freedom forced them to consider positive points of each method. Although King believed the philosophy of nonviolent direct action to be the most practical method, he understood why blacks would choose a violent direct action—the method employed by the radical slave preacher, Nathaniel Turner. In King's estimation, God was moving in the world. Black people simply had to bend their method to one which coincided with the overall personality of the divine, which was exhibited in the concept of agape love. If blacks did their part, as King understood it, certainly God would do the rest. King believed in a God of history—a God constantly engaged and operating in the affairs of humanity. Such an experience came with a caveat: blacks had to work together. Confrontation and agitation became cornerstones of his philosophy. In a similar vein, Du Bois believed that agitation was a good course of action as it aroused the true intent of social systems. "Agitation," as he saw it, "is a necessary evil to tell of the ills of the suffering. Without it many a nation has been lulled to false security and preened itself with virtues it did not possess."[14] Truth, therefore, is the issue of import. God's divine movement, according to King, has a way of eradicating anything that is contrary to love. This is the all powerful creator that King believed spoke to him, and encouraged him to continue to fight for justice.

Heritage was a very important element in King's life. One would be remiss to forget that King was the son, nephew, grandson, and great-grandson of Baptist preachers.[15] Operating at the intersection of religion and politics was not unfamiliar terrain for Dr. King. He was aware of his ministerial and social conscious pedigree, which extended back to his great-grandfather, Willis Williams. Williams was a charismatic slave preacher who used his

---

13. King, *Why We Can't Wait*, 123.
14. Du Bois, "Agitation," 1131–32.
15. Baldwin, *The Voice of Conscience*, 13.

gift of persuasion to recruit other slaves for church membership during a revival in 1855.[16] Willis and his wife, Lucrecia, gave birth to a baby boy, Adam Daniel Williams. A.D., as he was affectionally called, was attracted to the art of preaching at an early age. His imitation of his father and other slave preachers was often practiced to an audience of animals and/or children of the community.[17] The Reverend Parker Poullain mentored A.D. and licensed him to preach in 1888.[18] Five years later, he was called to pastor Ebenezer Baptist Church[19] in Atlanta, with a congregation consisting of only thirteen members. Like many other contemporary black ministers from similar backgrounds," says Clayborne Carson, "A.D. built his congregation by means of forceful preaching that addressed the everyday concerns of the poor and working class residents."[20] He was in discussion with prominent black leaders in the city regarding the injustices that many blacks so often experienced. A.D.'s social consciousness was at a high functioning level as he was a member of several prominent boards and organizations.[21] For instance, "he was president of the Atlanta Baptist Ministers' Union and treasurer of the National Baptist Convention, the most formidable ecclesiastical organization in black America;" additionally, "Williams emerged as an important city leader after the Atlanta race riot of 1906—a horrific affair involving white attacks on innocent blacks, fifty of whom lost their lives."[22] He believed in following both Du Bois' civil rights approach and Booker T. Washington's prescription for economic progression. He also made several

---

16. King, *Papers*, 1:2.
17. Ibid., 4.
18. Ibid.
19. Much of what King would come to know about God was via what is termed the *Ebenezer tradition*. Ebenezer was a place of intellectual stimulation and spiritual clarification. Its parishioners were proud to assert their authority as a community symbol and religious body. King often observed his father stand in the Ebenezer pulpit and *challenge the white supremacist values and institutions that attempted to silence his voice*. Such a sight must have forged a sense of pride—to see and hear his father command a crowd, and rally their resolve to always speak truth to power.
20. King, *Papers*, 1:7.
21. "Williams was a member of the Atlanta Baptist Ministers Union, chairman of both the executive board and the finance committee of the General State Baptist Convention, and a member of the Convention's educational board and its Baptist Young Peoples Union and Sunday School board." See King, *Papers*, 1:9.
22. Miller, *Voice of Deliverance*, 31.

prudent real estate deals that situated him and the King family financially in a more secure economic demographic.[23]

Martin Luther King, Sr. married the daughter of A.D., Alberta Christine Williams. Like his father-in-law, King, Sr. would graduate from Morehouse College and maintain a social consciousness that would eventually propel him into activism.

> Again, like Williams and many other black clergy, King, Sr., not only proclaimed racial equality, he also did something about it. In 1939 he led roughly a thousand demonstrators to Atlanta's City Hall, where they demanded the right to vote. The next year, he supported the protest of black teachers who wanted pay comparable to that of their white counterparts. He also provided leadership for the Atlanta Voters League. In the late 1940s he entered the City Hall of Atlanta and used elevators marked with signs reading "Whites Only." Soon the signs came down. For good reason, he became known as a "chronic complainer" about segregation.[24]

Interestingly enough, King, Sr. acquired his fiery, homiletically pew-walking prowess from watching and conversing with slave preachers.[25] Three generations removed from his slave preaching roots, King Jr. inherited a practice of always viewing governmental policy in light of his black social conscious heritage.[26] He became very active in the local NAACP[27] and he formed the Social and Political Action Committee at Dexter.[28] His social and political action committee plan read in part:

> [It] shall be established for the purpose of keeping the congregation intelligently informed concerning the social, political and economic situation. This committee shall keep before the congregation the importance of the N.A.A.C.P. The membership should unite with this great organization in a solid block. This committee shall also keep before the congregation the necessity of being registered voters. Every member of Dexter must be a registered voter. During elections, both state and national, this committee will

23. King, *Papers*, 1:11–13.
24. Ibid., 36.
25. Ibid., 35.
26. King, *Papers*, 2:30.
27. Ibid., 35.
28. Ibid., 34.

sponsor forums and mass meetings to discuss the relative merits of candidates and the major issues involved.[29]

Additionally, "King attended the monthly meetings of the Alabama Council on Human Relations, an affiliate of the Sothern Regional Council, the only significant interracial reform group in Montgomery. He also served briefly as the organization's vice president."[30] King Jr.'s black social consciousness was not only influenced by his family; extensive reading of Du Bois' work also provided a foundation for understanding the African American plight via study of African culture, customs, and traditions. As Lewis Baldwin notes, "Information concerning this aspect of the black religious past would have been accessible to him in the writings of scholars like W. E. B. Du Bois, whom he read closely."[31]

It is important to note that "King himself wrote about the *secret religious meetings* on the plantations, during which slaves *gained renewed faith* under the powerful and consolatory words of preachers."[32] Although King was familiar with the historical nexus between African peoples and African American existence via the experience of slavery, he never fully developed a mature understanding of how these connections between African religious traditions and such cultural transmissions were evident in the overall development of the twentieth-century black church.[33] In 1958 King published a response in *Ebony Magazine* to a question that was posed to him regarding a comparative analysis between Christianity and African religions. King answered in part:

> Christianity is an expression of the highest revelation of God. It is the synthesis of the best in all religions. In a sense Christianity is more valid than the tribal religions practiced by our African ancestors. This does not mean that these tribal religions are totally devoid of truth. It simply means that Christianity, while flowing through the streams of history, has incorporated the truths of all other religions and brought them together into meaningful and coherent system.[34]

---

29. Ibid., 290. (Recommendations to the Dexter Avenue Baptist Church for the Fiscal Year 1954–1955).
30. King, *Papers*, 2:34.
31. Baldwin, *Never to Leave Us Alone*, 15.
32 Ibid., 14–15.
33. Baldwin and Al-Hadid, *Between Cross and Crescent*, 13–25.
34. King, "Christianity and African Religions," 196.

King, at different times during his prophetic tenure, seems to unconsciously subscribe to westernized notions of religious dominance, while also affirming the African religious tradition as being relatively note worthy. In June of 1962, King gave an address at Zion Hill Baptist Church, in Los Angeles, California. King essentially says that the dilemma for blacks could be located primarily in their historical existence in America. King encourages his audience to "remember that it was in the year of 1619 when the first Negro slaves landed on the shores of the nation. They were brought here from the soils of Africa, and the Negro lived amid the system of slavery for 244 years."[35] In this address, King mentions Africa as a means of getting at what he considered to be the proper framework for understanding the plight of black Americans. But King does not necessarily acknowledge the heritage that was situated in the psyche of the first African slaves that were transported to the colonies. King does, however, surmise that the experience of slavery and the practice of "political domination, economic exploitation, segregation, and humiliation for well now 344 years"[36] demanded that oppressed blacks become intentional in responding to such a morally deprived experience. King furthers his plea by stating that, "He who gets behind in a race must forever remain behind or run faster than the man in front."[37] In a sense, King considered the fight for justice to entail a proper understanding of the *gaps of opportunity* that many African Americans failed to realize existed, at least within its proper historical context. The enslavement of African Americans created a pause in their intellectual development and maturity. While many whites benefited from cultural advancements and educational opportunities that were created as a result of slave labor, slaves were intentionally kept ignorant of such spaces. Slaves were effectively forced to succumb to thievery (for the mere necessities of life), and they also had to steal time, space, and resources in an attempt to learn a language and culture that held them captive. Existentially, King understands that the cultural delay in the African American experience had placed them in a rather precarious position. They did not have the luxury of isolation as seen in the practice of individualism; rather, says King, blacks have to perfect their individuality and "mobilize [their] resources and to

---

35. King, *Papers*, 7:476.
36. Ibid., 476–77.
37. Ibid., 477.

mobilize all of the constructive forces that [they] can muster to make a creative contribution in the life of our nation."[38]

Although he never visited South Africa, King believed that he and South Africans—like Arthur J. Luthuli[39] for instance—shared a common experience of oppression. King was aware of African splendor, and was proud of its traditions, but never truly grappled with how African religious thought created the here-and-now experience of the modern day black church. Although acquainted with the cultural synthesis of Du Bois' work, he never possessed Du Bois' understanding of the historical progression of black faith as seen in the experience of existential togetherness.

Yet King's familiarity with Du Bois' work is evident in a speech that King delivered in 1968 to celebrate Du Bois' hundredth birthday. He refers to Du Bois as "a man possessed of priceless dedication to his people."[40] He adds, "He virtually, before anyone else and more than anyone else, demolished the lies about Negroes in their most important and creative period of history. The truths he revealed are not yet the property of all Americans but they have been recorded and arm us for our contemporary battles."[41] According to King's expansive understanding of Du Boisian literature, although *Suppression of the African Slave Trade* and *The Philadelphia Negro* corrected the notion of an African American myth of inferiority, Du Bois' work would be of little use "without the mass involvement of Negroes."[42] Out of all the works by Du Bois, it seems as if King held Du Bois' *Black Reconstruction* in particularly high regard. It is in this work that King sees in Du Bois a pragmatically kindred spirit. Du Bois systematically dismantled previously established patterns of thought regarding the failure of Reconstruction. It was often posited within the scholarly community that the historical basis for explaining the *failure* of Reconstruction was situated in the experience of former slaves who lacked the ingenuity and intellect to adequately utilize political power. But as Du Bois' research shows, "Within five years the cotton crop had been restored and in the succeeding five years had exceeded prewar levels. At the same time other economic activity had ascended so rapidly [that] the rebirth of the South was almost completed."[43]

38. Ibid.
39. See Baldwin's, *Toward the Beloved Community*, 11.
40. King, "Honoring Dr. Du Bois," 118.
41. Ibid., 116.
42. Ibid., 115.
43. Ibid., 116–17.

What impressed King most, in my estimation, is the degree of dedication Du Bois exhibited throughout his career. For instance, *Black Reconstruction* alone took "six years in writing but thirty-three years in preparation."[44] The seriousness with which Du Bois devoted himself to truth impressed King. (Du Bois certainly had few intellectual equals of any color.)

Unlike Du Bois, however, King had a tendency to address issues using material that were not properly referenced. As Keith D. Miller outlines in his text, King *borrowed* material because it aptly illumed a truth that needed to be disseminated to the millions of psychologically enslaved African Americans who were suffering in America.[45] The practice of borrowing was well established within the black preaching tradition. King, as well as other prominent black preachers, understood material to be *re-usable* frameworks from which to validate and articulate their thoughts regarding the African American religious experience. He did, however, take entire passages from the work of other preachers and scholars. Miller notes that King borrowed from Phillip Brooks, the great abolitionist preacher, without proper acknowledgment, as he did also from George Buttrick's *Parables of Jesus*.[46] To be sure, King should have done a better job at providing accurate attribution for these works. But in King's case, it was not necessarily an issue of being *unoriginal*; rather, the construct of proper citation and reference was not a central theme in his early educational odyssey. It may be deduced from Patrick Parr's current work that one of King's Crozer Theological Seminary professors, George Davis, is particularly responsible for not correcting King's oftentimes blatant plagiarism, a responsibility that seems reasonably clear in part because King had "at least eight classes from Davis."[47]

While attending Crozer, King enrolled in a course taught by George Davis titled *Religious Development of Personality*. As a course assignment, King wrote a paper outlining his religious development titled *An Autobiography of Religious Development (1950)*.[48] In this work King reflects on his religious heritage and describes his initial call to ministry as an "inescapable drive" and "an inner urge calling me to serve humanity."[49] King also

44. Ibid., 116.
45. See Miller, *Voice of Deliverance*.
46. Ibid., 15.
47. Parr, *The Seminarian*, 181.
48. King, *Papers*, 1:360.
49. Ibid., 363.

acknowledges that "conversion for me was never an abrupt something. I have never experienced the so called crisis moment. Religion has just been something that I grew up in. Conversion for me has been the gradual intaking of the noble (ideals) set forth in my family and my environment, and I must admit that this intaking has been largely unconscious."[50] As Keith Miller contends, an attempt to understand the mind of King must go beyond his introduction to white graduate institutions.[51] One must review the commencement of the African American experience that, for King, is situated in the experience of slavery. King was certainly familiar with slave conversion narratives that his father certainly would have discussed with him as a child. His use of *abruptness* in reference to conversion could certainly imply an awareness of slave conversion comparison. A close reading of King's paper reveals a person who is deeply family and community oriented; he is also both confident and secure. Moreover, he displays a mature understanding of how intricately integrated religion is in his life. "In fact," he confidently concludes, "the two (religion and life) cannot be separated; religion for me is life."[52] King's notion of religion encompassed the whole of his existence. It was very difficult for him to differentiate any aspect of African American religious experience. This is not to presume that King had an advanced awareness of this interconnected reality. It seems as though King lacked the synthesis needed to interpret the origin of all of the nuances of black life that he so eloquently articulated. And this fact is perhaps what lends credence to a certain level of genius.

Privilege, Maturation, and Cultural Empathy

Prior to his move to Montgomery, King led a life of social privilege. The King family were middle-class people. This of course does not mean that they had no financial concerns, only that their financial status was much better than so many other black families. Although he was exposed to racism, his strong familial connection provided a cultural filter of sorts. When he vowed to hate all white people because of such exposure, his parents provided guidance regarding how to best process the experience. They did not deny him the emotional response; rather they simply redirected his

---

50. Ibid., 361.
51. Miller, *Voice of Deliverance*, 17.
52. King, *Papers*, 1:363.

response to fit the Christian ethic of love.⁵³ King grew up in the Deep South in the 1930s and 1940s. Considering the nefarious practices of Jim Crow, King's peer group would have consisted of several father-less children. But his home was one of warmth, love, and education. Early in life, King was developing the notion of his *somebody-ness*.

King went to Montgomery with a high sense of self-efficacy and religious training. A couple of months into the Montgomery Bus Boycott, King began receiving death threats—often thirty or forty calls would come in daily. This became the norm, and although aware that such threats might be carried out, King was never disturbed to the point of removing himself from his leadership position. On one particular occasion, however, King became fearful when he received a call late one night in 1956. He was informed that he had three days to get out of the city of Montgomery, or he would be killed and his home bombed. This particular message burdened King.

> I got out of bed and began to walk the floor. I had heard these things before, but for some reason that night it got to me. I turned over and I tried to go to sleep, but I couldn't sleep. I was frustrated, bewildered, and then I got up. Finally I went to the kitchen and heated a pot of coffee. I was ready to give up. With my cup of coffee sitting untouched before me I tried to think of a way to move out of the picture without appearing a coward.⁵⁴

This was the first time in King's life in which he was forced out of his privileged state. He surmised that *Something* was saying, "You can't call on Daddy now, you can't even call on Mama. You've got to call on that something in that person that your Daddy used to tell you about, that power that can make a way out of no way."⁵⁵ This experience was King's crisis moment. When he felt utterly vulnerable and dependent upon God, his prayer life would become the force that would ultimately sustain him throughout his ministry. King, Lewis Baldwin contends, had long been exposed to the African American prayer tradition,⁵⁶ but his notion of God acting as a Cosmic Companion would not come into full maturity until his involvement with the modern day civil rights movement. King was a preacher who craved the very essence of the divine; therefore, he developed the habit of communing

53. Ibid., 362.
54. King, *Autobiography*, 77.
55. Ibid.
56. Baldwin, *Never to Leave Us Alone*, 10–23.

with God on a continual basis. It was in these moments of deep communion with the divine that he garnered enough strength to continue to lead the black struggle in America. Along with his impressive education, prayer also informed how to respond to the reality of racial hatred. King ultimately viewed racism as a form of evil; racists were simply pawns used to promote such a celestial agenda. King learned that, therefore, human vices were futile as evil was a supernatural force that should initially be engaged via a more dominant supernatural force. He used prayer as a tactic to disarm such forces.

By the age of six, King had developed both a theoretical and practical understanding of racism. When informed that he and his white friend could no longer play together because he was black, and his friend, white, King became desperately upset and decided that he would, from that moment forward, hate white people. King admits that it was his parents who reminded him that love conquers hate, and that he should love all people because God loves them. This early experience in King's life prepared him to further this idea of agape love within the critical study of Personalism. This entails a belief that God sees God's self in the embodiment of every individual. Every human being, therefore, has intrinsic worth and value. King was attracted to the ideal of Personalism because its tenets matched emphases that were stressed in his community; for instance, ideas such as spirit, mind, will, love, and reason can all be traced to the ethos of African American slave culture. It is King's childhood and Morehouse experiences that provided an abstract example of Personalist philosophy. Although Crozer professor George Davis, and Boston University professor Edgar S. Brightman, enhanced King's theoretical understanding of humanity, he discovered the basic concept of human personality from a black cultural experience rather than white educational spaces. If the situation with his friend at the age of six inspired King to hate, an experience at the age of fifteen inspired him to commit to the idea of social change, and grapple with the notion of what it feels like to be treated as inferior.

On April 17, 1944, as a member of the Debate Team at Booker T. Washington High School, King traveled to Dublin, Georgia. The speech that he was to deliver that evening was titled *The Negro and the Constitution (1944)*. Patrick Parr contends that his speech was not of the religious type.[57] However, when analyzing the African American experience, one must remember that every experience is of the religious type as all black

---

57. Parr, *The Seminarian*, 2.

experiences share the existential concern of meaning and worth. King's speech was of the religious-type—due in part to a critique in how societal injustices de-value personality, which God has situated within the very essence of black people. King's speech also illumed the hypocritical notion of American democracy. A segment of its citizenry was stagnating due to the mighty *chains of oppression*. King and Hiram Kendall, a debate participant and classmate, were forced to give their seats to white passengers upon their return to Atlanta and were forced to stand for the duration of the ride. King, flustered from the experience, exclaimed, "that night will never leave my memory. It was the angriest I have ever been in my life. Suddenly I realized you don't count, you're nobody."[58]

Dr. King attempted to follow the Du Boisian trajectory of race-liberation. First, all falsehoods had to be forcefully and systematically refuted. A lie will remain a lie until it is exposed as a lie. Second, the people must collectively believe the truth. It is one thing to have access to information, but it is quite another to have information yet lack the understanding to take full advantage of such a truth. Truth plus mobilization produces social movements. Whereas Du Bois painstakingly uncovered the truth, King struggled to disseminate this truth to the masses and organize their bodies to agree with their newly informed minds. His message was one of love, community, and education. He taught the concept of togetherness; with it, they were unstoppable. Without it, they were doomed to a life of subjugation and isolation. He marched, endured police brutality, and was arrested twenty-six times. Due to his ability to bring black people together under the premise of liberation, King was brutally assassinated on April 4, 1968.

King's position of non-violence led several black leaders to think of him as weak and subservient, and that his methods of protest were ineffective and dangerous. King understood that violence against the white power structure would merely situate blacks in an even more hostile and vulnerable position. King adamantly believed that whites would like nothing more than to obtain justification for eradicating a whole race of people; therefore, he reasoned that "violence is impractical and that now, more than ever before, we must pursue the course of nonviolence to achieve a reign of justice and a rule of love in our society, and that hatred and violence must be cast into the unending limbo if we are to survive."[59] This thought was expressed in his dealing with all who promoted Black Nationalism. Being

---

58. Ibid., 5.
59. King, *Autobiography*, 269.

of a dialectical mindset, King critiqued not only Malcolm X, but all who promoted violence as a means of gaining equality for black people. Within his synthesis, however, he concluded that:

> In a real sense, the growth of Black Nationalism was symptomatic of the deeper unrest, discontent, and frustration of many Negroes because of the continued existence of racial discrimination. Black Nationalism was a way out of that dilemma. It was based on an unrealistic and sectional perspective that I condemned both publicly and privately. It substituted the tyranny of black supremacy for the tyranny of white supremacy. I always contended that we as a race must not seek to rise from a position of disadvantage to one of advantage, but to create a moral balance in society where democracy and brotherhood would be a reality for all men.[60]

King believed that opposing forces could work toward a common good. As was the case in African tradition, many tribes and nations served and worshipped their respective Gods. The unifying principle is seen in the ability to locate commonality in any situation. King would discover such commonality with Rosa Parks.

On December 1 1955, Rosa Parks, while riding a city bus home from a long day of work, was told that she needed to move to the back of the bus to make room for the white passengers. If Mrs. Parks followed the driver's command she would have to stand while a white male passenger, who had just boarded the bus, would sit. The other three Negro passengers immediately complied with the driver's request. But Mrs. Parks quietly refused. The result was her arrest.[61] As James Melvin Washington observes,

> Mrs. Park's refusal to move back was her intrepid affirmation that she had had enough. It was an individual expression of a timeless longing for human dignity and freedom. She was not "planted" there by the NAACP, or any other organization; she was planted there by her personal sense of dignity and self-respect. She was a victim of both the forces of history and the forces of destiny. She had been tracked down by the *Zeitgeist*—the spirit of the time.[62]

It is likely that King considered Rosa Parks' situation within the context of the bus experience of his youth. The sense of togetherness was formed by the commonality of their oppression. This shared experience elicited King's

---

60. Ibid.
61. King, "Stride toward Freedom," 420.
62. Ibid.

empathy and sympathy. It was enough to encourage him to correlate the synergy of historical events within religious notions of freedom. Dr. King concluded that no other black should endure such an experience.

It is interesting to note, however, that King had not always practiced such existential togetherness. While serving as assistant pastor at First Baptist of East Elmhurst, in Queens, as part of field study, King was tutored by William E. Gardner. Reverend Gardner, although impressed with King's intellectual abilities, nevertheless wrote an evaluation calling attention to King's lack of connectedness to the common *Negro*. It is clear that King's interaction with people in the community was interpreted as "aloofness," "smugness," and "snobbishness."[63] At this stage of development, King was still growing in many areas of his life, as would anybody of his age. He was privileged, but he would come to learn how to use that privilege for the benefit of others.

By 1955, as a maturing religious thinker, the onus was upon King's shoulders to assist in alleviating such experiences as he and Rosa Parks had to endure. In his work, *Strength to Love* (1963), King describes God as a Power who is able to intervene in human affairs. Knowing the heart of the people, King understood that doubt regarding God's care was often the result of experiencing the reality of existential isolation. But King reminds the reader that "God walks with us. He has placed within the very structure of this universe certain absolute moral laws. We can neither defy nor break them. If we disobey them, they will break us. The forces of evil may temporarily conquer truth, but truth will ultimately conquer its conqueror. Our God is able."[64] King's ability to reassure the black masses of God's faithfulness is reminiscent of Moses. So much so, according to Michael Eric Dyson, that

> [h]e was constantly told by a stream of well-wishers and followers that he was Moses or, sometimes, a Christ-like Messiah sent from God to do God's will. If King was convinced, like Jesus, that his death could be redemptive, it was not out of arrogance, like Jesus, that his death could be redemptive, it was not out of arrogance, but a hard-headed, clear-eyed belief that his martyrdom could drive home the very cause for which he was willing to die.[65]

---

63. Ibid., 172.
64. Ibid., 507.
65. Dyson, *I May Not Get There With You*, 303.

King was indeed willing to sacrifice his life for the cause of black equality. As a young man of comfort, King was afforded the luxury to observe, rather than be a victim of, perennial racism. As was the case with Moses' comfort, observational leadership would not suffice if liberation was to become a reality for the Hebrews. God required Moses to lead from the front, and Moses, according to King, was captured by divine influence and compelled to lead. King, like Moses, would have to endure the maturation process of a downtrodden people. Although he posits that his father "never made more than an ordinary salary,"[66] King, Sr. eventually became the highest paid black minister in Atlanta.[67] King possibly attempted to downplay his privilege as a means of associating with the *least of these* within the black community. As early as 1950, he attempted to convince those in his extended realm that he was a man of very humble means, but King's family ascension to privilege can be viewed as early as 1900 when A.D. and the Ebenezer congregation purchased a building that was previously owned by Fifth Baptist Church, a white congregation.[68]

The Burden of God

I presume that every reasonable human being is likely to acknowledge a burden in at least one area of life. In this life we are all burdened—some more than others, but the reality is we all have personal loads to bear. These types of loads I refer to as existential burdens. We attempt to make sense of their meaning and purpose in life. At times, we conquer some of these burdens. Some existential philosophers would posit that it is the human will that allows such an experience—it is the human will that arises from the ashes as a new phoenix of joy and relief. This may very well be true; occasionally, we do overcome existential burdens. But there is another type of burden that refuses to go away. When God puts God's hands on a prophet, it is too heavy to be moved. This simply means that a person called by God does not easily reject such a calling. Although burdensome, the prophet is able to endure tremendous stress as the *Spirit of the Lord* is assisting in the work.

Abraham Heschel declares that compassion for humanity and sympathy for God is what burdens the prophet. In other words, when God hurts,

66. King, *Papers*, 1:360.
67. Ibid., 31.
68. Ibid., 9.

the prophet hurts. The prophet is so intertwined with the reality of the divine that God's feelings become the expressed Word of God through the prophet. God's ultimate ethic always calls for what is just and right. When God feels the tragic moans of an oppressed people, God calls the prophet to remedy the situation: For God says, *I have heard the cries due to their suffering, and I am concerned. Moses, go down and tell Pharaoh to let My people go.* God's concern, by default, becomes the Prophet's concern. God's burden, becomes the prophet's burden.

That same divine concern and burden was in Memphis in 1968. King went there because God's burden was upon him. God was there with the 1300 sanitation workers who collectively decided that they had value. During a bad storm on Feb 1, two black sanitation workers were killed when the garbage compacter was triggered by accident; on that same day 22 black workers were sent home without pay, but their white supervisors were allowed to stay, with pay. On February 12 the black workers officially went on strike for better safety guidelines and equal pay. As King was flying across the nation giving talks, he received a call from James Lawson indicating that he was needed in Memphis. When King got there, he reminded the sanitation workers that power concedes nothing without a demand. And he commended them for standing up for what is right—even if it meant losing their jobs. If the people desired value, they had to first value themselves, and then protest for the right to be treated with value and dignity from others.

While flying into Memphis, King was aware of a bomb threat. He was aware that close acquaintances questioned his stance regarding the Poor People's Campaign, that the FBI had him under surveillance, and that the black power leadership was attempting to usurp his nonviolent direct action philosophy. He understood that the ominous weather conditions were tantamount to the darkness that had for so long engulfed the consciousness of the nation. Even in the face of internal and external opposition, a prophet must preach. King was burdened with a Word. Moreover, after delivering a powerful speech, the people were encouraged to fight on. The next day, as King stepped out of room 306 onto the balcony at the Lorraine Hotel, he was engaged in banter, and the last words he would utter on this side of eternity would be a request for a musician to play *Precious Lord, Take my Hand.* After making his request, a bullet ripped through his jaw. The prophet was dead before the ambulance reached the hospital. He had had a sense that his end was near. Just a month earlier he had preached his own funeral. On that day, he told his audience that he did not want a long funeral, he did not want the preacher to take too long, he didn't want them to mention his education, awards, and accolades. He wanted them to mention that he tried to give his life serving others.[69]

God had allowed King to live long enough to see the hope for which African Americans continue to strive. It is difficult to fight against white oppression and black oppression simultaneously, but King did both. The same spirit that burdened King is the same spirit that burdened the itinerant preacher from Galilee. Jesus, too, was burdened with a Word. He went preaching the love of God to the least of these. He preached in the Synagogue. He preached the Word to a demon possessed man. He preached against a Roman and Jewish system of domination. He preached until they decided that enough is enough—the prophet had to die.

It is often posited that the greatest sermon Jesus ever preached was his life. I suppose this is true when one considers his homiletical *close* (He simply said, *it is finished.*). The work for African American equality, however, is ripe for attention and action. Dr. King's death left a void in black consciousness; although his popularity was declining; King still wielded influence. For many, he was still the thread that held together the multilayered pieces of the African American garb. A generation was arising with militant notions of fighting for black equality. Dr. King opposed this position because, in his estimation, the result would be the annihilation of the black race in America. He also believed that violence only creates an appetite for more violence; even if blacks were miraculously victorious, the exposure to such levels of violence would damage the human mind and soul, and corrupt the personality that God had created. With damaged psyches, blacks would be unable to foster a sense of community and lose their intimacy and mutual vulnerability.

Analysis of Dr. King's Existential Togetherness Rhetoric

For thirteen years, King was fairly certain that he would be killed for his work. In a rather peculiar way, King understood that his demise would not occur due to old age; rather, much like John F. Kennedy and many other well known (as well as lesser known) social justice advocates, his life would come to an abrupt end via violent means. Just two months before his assassination, King preached a sermon titled *The Drum Major Instinct*

---

69. King, "Drum Major Instinct," 253–64.

(1968). Before King began to talk about death, and the high probability of his demise and subsequent funeral, he described the church as an organism of unconditional acceptance. Such a space is devoid of bravado and unsubstantiated arrogance:

> And the church is the one place where a doctor ought to forget that he's a doctor. The church is the one place where a PhD ought to forget that he's a PhD. The church is the one place that the school teacher ought to forget the degree she has behind her name. The church is the one place where the lawyer ought to forget that he's a lawyer. And any church that violates the "whosoever will, let him come" doctrine is a dead, cold church, and nothing but a little social club with a thin veneer of religiosity. When the church is true to its nature, it says, "Whosoever will, let him come." And it is not supposed to satisfy the perverted uses of the drum major instinct. It's the one place where everybody should be the same, standing before a common master and savior. And a recognition grows out of this—that all men are brothers because they are children of a common father.[70]

A Kingian church model entails an appreciation for all human life. It does not matter the degree of nuance associated with individual lifestyles and occupations. The Church is where all of God's children get together and form a bond of religious solidarity. King understood that the natural order of the Church meant it did not always rise to the occasion. In such an event, the prophet was responsible for reiterating the proper order of things. Advocacy is needed for those overwhelmed by systems that seem to oppress God's natural order of liberation for all human beings. Due to his advocacy for African Americans and other marginalized groups in America, and the world, King was constantly living under the threat of death. In 1958 Mrs. Izola Curry came close to ending Dr. King's life while he was autographing his newly released narrative of the Montgomery Movement (*Stride Toward Freedom*). But in 1958, I am not sure whether King had conceptualized what would come to be known as his *Promised Land Vision*. Fast forward ten years, however, and one finds a much more spiritually mature King. He went to Memphis, Tennessee with an inkling that perhaps death was closer than it had ever been. On April 3, 1968, Dr. Martin Luther King Jr., although ill, went to Bishop Charles Mason Temple Church and spoke to an overflowing crowd of supporters. His speech for the evening was titled:

---

70. Ibid., 258–59.

I've Been to the Mountain Top. It would be the last time that he would stand and deliver a prophetic oration before a crowd. Dr. King's *I've been to the Mountain Top* speech/sermon is reminiscent of Moses' farewell address to the Hebrews.

Moses, a man to whom God spoke face to face, at the tender age of 120 had come to the end of his prophetic life. In a Gibranian[71] manner, Moses has a rather fascinating resume. He delivered the Israelites from Egyptian slavery. He was their leader as they wandered in the Wilderness for forty years. He fed them when they were hungry, and intervened on their behalf when God considered killing them. As he marched the Israelites to the borders of Canaan, he understood that God would not allow him to cross over into the Promised Land. Rather, God had allowed him to climb Mount Nebo, and from this elevated position, Moses looked over and saw all that awaited his people—all that God had promised. Though he would not lead them into the Promised Land, God did allow him to see God's faithfulness before he died. And after coming down from this spiritual experience, encamped in Moab, where the Jordan River flows into the Dead Sea, Moses prepared to deliver his final sermon to God's people. The old generation had perished in the wilderness, and Moses wanted to be sure that the new generation understood God's Law. Before his demise, Moses wanted them to know and remember what God had done. Because he knew that he would never see them again, the prophet was burdened to leave a Word. In a similar manner, King's rhetoric focuses on what it will take for African Americans to survive what awaits them in their Promised Land.

---

71. In Kahlil Gibran's *The Prophet*, an erudite traveler by the name of Almustafa dwelt in the city of Orphalese for twelve years. While in the city, he became renowned as a man of great philosophical insight; a man filled with the wisdom of God. But much to the dismay of the citizens in this great city, this man who had come to be known as *The Prophet* one day ascertains that his time among this beloved community has come to an end. And with a sense of departure at hand, the Spirit moves him to climb the city walls, and along the horizon he sees his ship approaching with the primary purpose of taking him back to his home land. As he makes his way to the city border, the people cease tending the fields. Every shop in the Market Square closes—and every person in the city follows Almustafa to the border. They know that he must depart, but before he leaves, they request that he leave them with a Word. A woman by the name of Almitra is the first to make a request. She asks him to speak on the topic of love. He honors her request and recommends, "When love beckons to you; although her ways are hard, one must follow." Other requests are submitted; and Almustafa speaks on a range of topics (joy and sorrow; reason and passion, religion; pain; friendship, et al). Finally, when the questions stopped and tears ceased falling down their faces, Almustafa has nothing else to give, so he boards his ship and sails into the evening sunset. See Gibran, *The Prophet*.

Existential Togetherness

While highlighting the importance of allowing God to perform wondrous works on behalf of African Americans, blacks had to also be willing to work with one another to bring about a better future. King envisioned that, with the proper preparation, *"We have an opportunity to make America a better nation."*[72] But such a vision would require understanding the God of history, establishing a relevant ministry, and adhering to notions of existential togetherness.

Theme One: God of History

Despite the many injustices occurring in America in 1968, King nevertheless believed that God was still in control. God was still his cosmic companion, even if he felt that "the nation is sick. Trouble is in the land. Confusion all around."[73] The nation was certainly sick. The United States not only exhibited sick tendencies at home via acts of racial violence and oppression; its sickness had spread into the realm of international relations.

In February of 1967, at the Nation Institute in Los Angeles, King gave a talk on the subject of "The Casualties of the War in Vietnam." He said in part.

> Some one million Vietnamese children have been casualties of this brutal war. A war in which children are incinerated by napalm, in which American soldiers die in mounting numbers while other American soldiers, according to press accounts, in unrestrained hatred shoot the wounded enemy as they lie on the ground, is a war that mutilates the conscience. These causalities are enough to cause all men to rise up with righteous indignation and oppose the very nature of this war.[74]

Although King understood that the current president, Lyndon B. Johnson, was an aggressive advocate for the Civil Rights Bill (1964), his conscience nevertheless compelled him to speak out against the administration and declared that "a brief look at the background and history of this war reveals with brutal clarity the ugliness of our policy."[75] On April 4, in the same year, King gave a speech titled "Beyond Vietnam: A Time to Break Silence" at Riverside Church in New York City. It is in this space that King

---

72. King, "I've Been to the Mountain Top," 273.
73. Ibid., 266.
74. King, "The Casualties of the War in Vietnam," 100.
75. Ibid., 101.

presented a rationale for becoming vocal against the United States' involvement in Vietnam. King had seen much hope in President Johnson's involvement and backing of the Poverty Program. This program was of the utmost concern for King as it focused on eradicating economic disparities among both poor black and whites. The US involvement in the war, however, pulled resources from the Poverty Program and halted all economic progress for the marginalized in American society. Additionally, King observed that the US government was "taking the black young men who had been crippled by our society and sending them 8,000 miles away to guarantee liberties in Southeast Asia which they had not found in Southwest Georgia and East Harlem."[76] King discovered his own hypocrisy in remaining silent. Yet he could no longer ignore his criticisms of urban blacks and their violent methods of protest without also condemning the violence that his country promoted in other corners of the globe. As a preacher and Nobel Laureate, King resolved "to work harder than I had ever worked before for "the brotherhood of man."[77] This was an unpopular move for King. As a result of his public stance, he lost the support of liberal whites, as well as blacks who aligned themselves with Lyndon B. Johnson and his administration. King, however, believed that he had a moral obligation to resist evil, wherever it was discovered. The War in Vietnam, along with the Poor People's Campaign, must have weighed heavily on his mind during this period.

King rationalized that God, as Supreme Personality, was somehow moving God's divine hand, and shaping the world to fit a divine purpose. In other words, the presence of evil and chaos does not provide *a priori* evidence that God is unconcerned and inactive in the affairs of humanity. Rather, King notes: "I know, somehow, that only when it is dark enough, can you see the stars. And I see God working in this period of the twentieth century in a way that men, in some strange way, are responding—something is happening in our world."[78] That something to which King refers is that unified cry among opposed peoples that freedom is the preferred option for their existence. And he does not simply relegate such an experience to that of African Americans. He says that Africans, as well, are tired of oppressive states of being; therefore, "the masses of people are rising up. And whenever they are assembled today, whether they are in Johannesburg, South Africa; Nairobi, Kenya; Accra, Ghana; New York City; Atlanta,

---

76. King, "Beyond Vietnam," 204.
77. Ibid., 205.
78. King, "I've Been to the Mountain Top," 266.

Georgia; Jackson, Mississippi; or Memphis, Tennessee—the cry is always the same—'We want to be free.'"[79]

King had mastered this notion of a God in history while matriculating through his graduate school programs. George Davis, for instance, described the God of history as a *Working, toiling God*. Davis interpreted God as the Supreme Personality who rides the *tides of history*.[80] Such thinking is certainly in accordance with King's orientation of evangelical liberalism. King would come to terms with the God in history via observation of God's *Creative Power*.[81] King's God was powerful enough to direct events in history, as William Whatley asserts.[82] God was not a deistic being unconcerned with creation; rather, the God of history was constantly moving and directing the affairs of humanity. This type of power was responsible for unfolding the events of the civil rights movement, and King's ultimate demise.

King understood that his life had been consistently targeted since his emergence as the leader of the Montgomery Movement. But God had allowed him, as he so eloquently presents, *to live in this period, to see what is unfolding*.[83] Divine involvement in human affairs, however, does not always translate into the human moment of expediency. By 1968, the world seemed to contradict God's promotion of moral order. War was in the land. The American people were therefore engaged in conflict on two fronts. They had to contend with the mistreatment of African Americans at home, and grapple morally with sending those same oppressed people to fight for equality and justice in a land not their own. Black radicalism was also on the rise. The people were tired of waiting on the God of History. History had been unfair to the majority of blacks in America. In fact, blacks were fighting for equity and equality as a result of the historical movement of slavery. However, many failed to grasp fully the notion of existential freedom as seen in human lived experience. Although a creative, loving, and engaged God was in control of history, human beings were free to choose to conform to the loving nature of God through their interactions with others, or deny self-worth by negating the divine heritage of personality in other human beings. The latter position is what created tension between black radicals of the movement and those, like King, who wholeheartedly

---

79. Ibid., 267.
80. Ansbro, *Martin Luther King, Jr.*, 63.
81. Whatley, *Roots of Resistance*, 25.
82. King, "I've Been to the Mountain Top," 266.
83. Ibid., 267.

subscribed to liberal evangelicalism. It was the preachers' responsibility, in King's estimation, to assist in properly bringing to the forefront this reality of a God who, despite human perception and logic, still works on behalf of the oppressed of society. In a sense, the inability to do so often caused King to become extremely critical of clergy, both black and white.

Dr. King was reared in a social milieu in which the black preacher was the *de facto* leader of the black community. As early as he could remember, from his family records and other historical accounts, the black preacher had been responsible for providing social, political, and religious instruction to oppressed blacks in America. As a boy, King was exposed to some of the most erudite black ministers in the country. They were college professors, presidents, pastors, businesspersons, civic leaders, and so on. The great tradition of black protest, for King, was situated within the Black Church. Extending back four generations, the King family had been actively leading black people in the arena of social agitation. It is not surprising, then, in Du Boisian manner, King rhetorically asked, "Who is it that is supposed to articulate the longings and aspirations of the people more than the preacher?"[84]

The major charge that King would lay before his fellow clergy would be that of being dialectically dishonest. King took issue, as was the case with slave preachers, with the notion of preaching about an existence in the here-and-now without balancing such a suggestion with messages of the *otherworldly*. Conversely, he also took issue with those who preached the *otherworldly* and neglected to articulate the kingdom of God in the here-and-now. It is small wonder that he would claim that "It's all right to talk about the new Jerusalem, but one day, God's preacher must talk about the New York, the new Atlanta, the new Philadelphia, the new Los Angeles, the new Memphis, Tennessee. This is what we have to do."[85] A relevant ministry, then, is comprised of a balanced understanding of how the God of history works with people in the here-and-now to create better living conditions for all human beings. During the civil rights movement, King felt the need to confront black clergy who remained silent and inactive; as he understood it, the preacher was responsible for alerting the people to the movement of God. Dr. King sensed that God was unfolding events in history that would ultimately lead to a better social situation for blacks in America, but knew that such a historical progression would require sacrifice.

84. Ibid., 269.
85. Ibid., 270.

Theme Two: Black Unity

Although he exhibited it in uncanny fashion, King did not fully understand the theoretical background of existential togetherness. King's formative years did not consist of analyzing the historical value of slave culture and African American continuity. He presumed that the slave preacher "had never heard of Plato or Aristotle. He would never have understood Einstein's theory of relativity."[86] This was not quite the case. Although he envisioned the slave preacher as the driving force for the community, King perhaps believed that the majority of slave preachers were unlearned, thereby, lacking a key requirement that had advanced King family ministers for nearly one hundred years. Although a gifted Baptist preacher, King was also a scholar. He was a man of deep thought—a brilliant thinker. His scholarly gaze assisted in providing frameworks and structure to think through what he had been grappling with via familial interaction and engagement. This combination made notions of human personality much easier to comprehend. Although King stressed the significance of all human personality, he never fully grasped the historic continuity between African and African American culture. Rather than commence existential togetherness within an African context, King and many others believed that African American culture was solely the result of American acculturation. Nevertheless, his *Mountaintop* speech is a clear indication that togetherness, as people of African descent living on American soil, was a major concern for him. He envisioned the mighty hand of God setting the stage for a divine act of justice. With or without evidence, African Americans should, according to King, have faith that God is working in history; they should be working as well. King pushed his listeners to consider the gravity of the experience by suggesting that "Now, what does all of this mean in this great period of history? It means that we've got to stay together. We've got to stay together and maintain unity."[87]

In his speech, King uses parallelism to connect with his audience in the most intimate of ways. For instance, he posits, "When the slaves get together, that's the beginning of getting out of slavery. Now let us maintain unity."[88] The former is in reference to the Exodus narrative. He presented the fact that Pharaoh kept the Hebrews enslaved by creating a scenario in which

---

86. King, *Papers*, 7:477.
87. Ibid., 267.
88. Ibid.

they fought amongst one another. King desired to move African Americans from the norm of individualism to a more integrated meaning of community within the practice of individuality. King urged his listeners "never [to] stop and forget that collectively, that means all of us together, collectively we are richer than all the nations in the world, with the exception of nine." He further states, "That's power right there, if we know how to pool it."[89] This, of course, is an African practice that King may have neglected as being a universal concept. Regardless, the point that King is attempting to convey is that the oppressor (i.e., white America) desires blacks to focus on issues that are not germane to the purpose for which they so readily assembled. In order to survive as a people, King said they needed togetherness. Dr. King's theory regarding the black condition in America failed to take into account, however, the earliest experience of enslaved Africans in the colonies via their African heritage. King does, however, understand that the lack of educational and cultural opportunities for over 344 years was detrimental to the advancement of the race. He therefore concludes that blacks need to "be concerned about your brother [and sister]. You may not be on strike. But either we go up together, or we go down together."[90] His use of the word brother is universal in nature. He is referring to a communal aspect of African existence. A marvelous element of the civil rights movement is that King was able to bring together black people from all fields of human endeavor. Black clergy are not afforded the privilege to look at the black prostitute with scorn or contempt. His/her failure to gain a decent footing in this society is the collective responsibility of all black persons who can be genetically connected to a particular African heritage via oppression. The same can be said of black transgendered, homosexual, lesbian, agnostic, atheist, Muslim persons, and so on. Although individual success is helpful, it is not enough to lift the black masses to a state of realistic cultural competition and competency. As such, systems that block access to white dominated cultural spaces must be identified and eradicated for all who are black.

Prayer and song have been perennial elements of black life for thousands of years. King and his colleagues appropriated slave songs to match their circumstances in the twentieth century. And as the slaves once stood and sat in circles to pray, so too did the civil rights protestors in their modern day baracoons. King would attest that singing and praying had a way of

---

89. Ibid., 270.
90. King, "I've Been to the Mountain Top," 273.

collectively strengthening the voice of an oppressed people. Some oppressors began to take note of the soulful cries of people who wanted to be free. "And every now and then we'd get in jail, and we'd see the jailers looking through the windows being moved by our prayers, and being moved by our words and our songs."[91] The African ring shout is also seen in the practice of what is known as the prayer circle. Much like the ring-shout, the prayer circle was another means of illustrating the togetherness of a group. The participants held hands and took turn praying for one another. King and other activists found solace in such spaces, which is why it was so often employed in the home, office, church, and jail cells. King practiced a common religious heritage that was not readily observable during his tenure; nevertheless, even in death, King would assert that he would remain with his people. Like his ancestors of yore, he would remain with the black masses in spirit, guiding them along their journey of life. "I may not get there with you. But I want you to know tonight, that we, as a people, will get to the promised land."[92]

King did not rhetorically correlate his incarceration experience with that of Africans being shackled together in the belly of a slave ship, but his use of imagery to describe the experience provides a context of cultural inference. If one was arrested during the civil rights movement, it is highly likely that such a person was a part of a larger detained group. Particularly during the Birmingham Campaign, "there were 2,500 demonstrators in jail at one time, a large proportion of them young people."[93] Considering this number, one can easily understand why King would suggest that sometimes the horde of black bodies in paddy wagons would render individual movement virtually impossible. He would reflect on such an experience by positing that, "and then we would be thrown in the paddy wagons, and sometimes we were stacked in there like sardines in a can."[94] In this state of togetherness, whether gay, heterosexual, woman, man, dark-skinned, light-skinned, poor, or rich, blacks were bonded together as a result of oppression. This is the only factor that matters when one is existentially bonded to another by a single common denominator of unfair treatment. For King, the onus of moral responsibility was upon the Church, in particular the Black Church, to assist in eradicating spaces of bias and unfair treatment.

91. Ibid.
92. Ibid., 275.
93. King, *Autobiography*, 208.
94. King, "I've Been to the Mountain Top," 269.

MLK Jr. & the Rhetoric of Existential Togetherness

In 1958, a young boy submitted a rather penetrating question to Dr. King's Ebony Magazine's *Advice for Living* column. The boy revealed that he was experiencing a rather strong attraction to other young boys, rather than developing a *normal* attraction for young girls. He presented this experience as a problem, and wondered if Dr. King could assist in directing him in the right direction for help. King responded by suggesting that his affinity toward the same sex was some sort of psychological response to *past experiences*. His advice, therefore, was for the young boy to seek a psychiatrist who was knowledgeable in the area of this type of identity conflict. King's response does not necessarily display abhorrence toward homosexuality; rather, I presume King's response can be understood contextually to align with the young man's desire to change the way he feels romantically about the same-sex. Because the young boy was not comfortable with his sexual urges, King may have deduced that his early environment exposed him to premature sexual experiences, which ultimately created a physiological need for the here-and-now experience. Thus, I contend that King viewed homosexuality within two paradigms: 1) There is an innate affinity toward the same sex (e.g., one is birthed into such a state). 2) Pre-mature environmental exposure to same–sex orientation creates a physiological affinity toward the same-sex (e.g., one is conditioned to exist in such a state). It seems to me that King's view on homosexuality was in essence dialectically rendered. His position may have shifted based on the context of the aforementioned paradigms. Regardless, King believed that both experiences ought to be appreciated and accepted within the context of God's beloved community.

Unfortunately, the Black Church has struggled to grapple effectively with the issue of same-sex relations within a Kingian model of acceptance. I submit that nearly every black church is comprised of persons who identify as extensions of the LGBTQ community. Some have garnered courage and boldly pronounced their identification, while others linger in the shadows anticipating the day when the Black Church will embrace them without equivocation. I find it interesting that the Black Church, as a moral authority, adheres to an unspoken policy of acceptance for LGBTQ so long as the experience of identity remains unknown. This, of course, is hypocritical and antithetical to Jesus' ethic of unconditional positive regard.

Victor Anderson notably takes issue with the moral legitimacy of an institution that has not embraced fully its LGBTQ members.[95] The failure

---

95. Anderson, *Creative Exchange*, 156.

of the Black Church to embrace all blacks, regardless of sexual orientation and lifestyle, has caused some blacks to consider the notion of community as being merely imaginative, hypocritical, and irrelevant. Anderson is correct in his ethical critique of a phenomenon that arbitrarily sets claims as to what is acceptable and unacceptable within the black communal religious politic. Sexual orientation was not an issue when slaves were shackled and placed in the belly of the slave ship; therefore, it should not be a current issue as blacks are struggling together in a country that still places shackles on them both physically and psychologically. The primary concern should be that of survival and progression, rather than the nature of black sexual affinity. Other African American religious scholars are correct, however, in interpreting the Black Church as more than an Apollonian myth, as Victor Anderson so eloquently describes it. Although the Black Church is a flawed organism, it has nevertheless provided a context of meaning and purpose for many generations of blacks in this country. In Kingian fashion, the Black Church must be understood within the framework of both/and, rather than an either/or paradigm. Depicting the Black Church as an heroic figure is appropriate as it has assisted in the maintenance and sustainability of black life for many a generation. The Black Church, as King envisioned it, has been, and needs to remain, a heroic symbol for a people seeking purpose and a sense of place in God's world. Again, however, Anderson is correct in questioning whether the Kingian notion of the Black Church can sufficiently address the needs and concerns of contemporary black life. Since the death of King, the Black Church has failed to provide an observable model of leadership as viewed in the experience of slave preaching tradition and praxis. To be sure, black clergy have been involved in the practice of black Christian individualism, but there has not been a high level of activism in which black people—regardless of religious belief, sexual orientation, or social classification—become united in a prolonged struggle to eradicate common injustices within the black community. The issues of mass incarceration and police shootings, for instance, are currently being addressed by various black organizations and leaders, but the Black Church has not organized beyond a stance of reactionary protest. Reactionary protest simply acknowledges that an injustice has occurred (and that such an injustice should cease to exist). Some leaders may hold press conferences as a means of alerting displeasure to such injustices; additionally, protest in the form of gatherings and marches are utilized to voice discontent. Unfortunately, reactionary protest does not cause enough agitation to arouse the conscience of a morally corrupt nation. Reactionary protest is beneficial in so far as it alerts people to the issue of injustice, but falls short in terms of eradicating the systemic nature of such moral evils. In this regard, the Black Church has failed to live up to the prophetic tradition of social activism as displayed in the slave preaching tradition that so readily embodied King and others during the civil rights movement. If African Americans are to survive this age of mass incarceration and police initiated killings, they must learn to work together toward a common goal of social progression for the whole of black life; and in my estimation, black men and woman who operate in the tradition of their slave preaching forebears should lead this effort.

Epilogue

Black Privilege—
The Antithesis to Existential Togetherness

Existential Togetherness was formed in the belly of the slave ship. It was in this dark and tortuous space where differentiated Africans shared both a common struggle and common enemy. Survival was experienced dialectically. On the one hand, some enslaved Africans forged bonds with other enslaved Africans and created a new reality of being. They may have been enemies while situated in their respective tribes in Africa, but the American experience of chattel slavery forced them to expand personal boundaries and cross—pollinate with others as a means of survival. On the other hand, some Africans desired distance from this newly identified communal group. Group classification, as they perceived it, limited their individual resources; therefore, they sought distinction as a means of setting themselves above the many, thus becoming the designated privileged few within the group. Du Bois observed this experience within the black masses in Philadelphia. Because of being denied access to white privilege, a new black aristocracy was birthed and thus created a space from which black leadership could potentially lead the masses to a better social standing. Such an approach, however, blurred the newly established line that rendered the masses at the mercy of the upper class. Privileged blacks, then, argues Du Bois, "refuse[d] to head any race movement on the plea that thus they draw the very color line against which they protest."[1] In essence, the idea of promoting equality for all blacks limited the amount of resources

---

1. Du Bois, *The Philadelphia Negro*, 178.

available to those who already held positions of power. In order to maintain privilege, opportunity of advancement must be denied to the mass majority.

Because white males possessed power, control, and influence over the lives of slaves, some slaves were lured into the seductive attraction of this privilege and appropriated it to fit into the limited experience of being enslaved. Black privilege was not birthed in the slave experience, as was the case with existential togetherness; rather, a degree of black privilege existed in pre-slavery African culture. In the latter part of the 15th century, the King of Benin informed Christian missionaries, for instance, that he would sell his servants into slavery for a white wife.[2] This king did not hold the notion of existential togetherness within his overall ethos. His privileged state only allowed him to consider spaces of opportunity and advancement. The African king, much like his European counterparts, possessed a degree of power, control, and influence over people. Rather than use his privilege to assist in the development of well-being for his people, the King of Benin used his people as a means to achieve the end of personal gratification.

I presume that the experience of slavery may have altered some African notions of privilege. Nevertheless, the idea of dominance, regardless the context, seems to be a perennial theme within black culture. It could certainly be argued that this is the case in virtually all known societies of the world. Some people, regardless of cultural affiliation, have a tendency to desire power, control, and position. Privilege, at its core, seems to be a human issue rather than simply a racial tendency. I understand why some blacks have difficulty accepting the notion of black privilege. The black experience in America has been one of perennial struggle and suffering. A lot of the dysfunction within the African American community can, perhaps, be traced to elements of racism that came into being centuries ago. To be sure, blacks living in the twenty-first century United States are bequeathed a legacy of racial inequality. And because of the constant struggle for survival, some blacks have chosen to disregard community in an effort to subscribe to notions of privileged individualism. This mode of thinking permeates deep within black group sub–consciousness. For instance, the 1990's Hip Hop culture is evident of the unconscious response of blacks who desire to take from other blacks as a means of self-elevation.[3] In his song "Gimme the Loot," Christopher Wallace (A.K.A The Notorious B.I.G.)

---

2. Williams, *History of the Negro Race*, chapter 4.

3. The Notorious B.I.G., "Gimme the Loot," lines 18–19, genius.com/The-notorious-big-gimme-the-loot-lyrics.

Epilogue

says, "Nigga, you ain't got to explain shit. I've been robbing motherfuckas since the slave ships." His rhetoric is a rather candid and uncanny display of historical affiliation to a legacy of abused black privilege. His mode of survival coincides with ancestors who may have been complicit in slaveship division. To be sure, the trek of the Middle Passage would have allowed time for social networks to be formed; and within every social network there exists degrees of stratification. Such a perception of black individualism has weakened the progressive movement of blacks for centuries. Such an experience, however, aids in understanding fully how privilege can be nuanced even within spaces that are controlled by stronger elements of influence, power, and control.

Peggy McIntosh's analysis of white privilege is a wonderful illustration of how privilege is both nuanced and stratified. Her objective, as a white female scholar, was to observe ways in which white male privilege prevented white females from potentially living free from male influence, power, and control. Notwithstanding her justifiable critique, she nuanced gendered privilege and considered how race privilege stratifies a particular group above another. McIntosh also considers how her *white privilege* has gone unchecked and virtually unexamined. The lack of historical understanding of the African American slave experience, she argues, hindered her from gaining an appreciation for the African American social plight.[4] Her willingness to embrace her white privilege, however, afforded enough intellectual space to consider a detachment from the lived experience of a race of people that she likely encountered on a regular basis.

Although acting as a marginalized group within the American social structure, blacks nonetheless adapted to a smaller scale of privilege, which is based on subordination to white privilege. Black privilege, then, is the metaphorical cousin of white privilege. An early trace of whiteness is found in the operative use of black privilege. Joseph Holloway asserts, for instance, that during slavery, "also in the 1800s a movement was started by blacks who worked as house servants, many of whom had white as well as black forebears. The term colored was used by these offspring to distinguish themselves from the Africans who worked in the fields."[5] This movement of social stratification attempted to elevate one group within an oppressed system over another within the same oppressed setting. Although black privilege does not reach the degree to which white privilege dominates the

---

4 McIntosh, *White Privilege and Male Privilege*, lines 6–10.

5. Holloway, *Africanisms in American Culture*, xix.

world, it nevertheless strives to come as close to white representation as possible. Holloway goes on to argue that "the Brown Fellowship," which was founded in 1794, "was established, admitting members of mixed heritage." Holloway further posits that "a similar society in New Orleans was called the Blue Vein Society; membership was based on skin color so light that the blue veins could be seen."[6]

Lawrence Otis Graham states that in 1968, his Great-grandmother, as a member of the blue veined crowd, did not possess a concern for the experience of suffering among blacks that she often saw on television.[7] In fact, according to Graham, she was against cultural norms of black life such as music; she perhaps believed that such a heritage was attached to the experience of slavery.[8] In essence, she wanted to be associated with something other than a slave heritage. She desired to be identified as American, rather than African American.

Reinhold Niebuhr is correct in stating that "inequalities of social privilege develop in every society, and that these inequalities become the basis of class divisions and class solidarity."[9] African privilege was based on the desire to possess and expand beyond one's own geographical location. Such a desire was tantamount to the European quest to insert themselves at the very center of global domination. This position gave them a 360-degree vantage point of control and privilege over other peoples of the world. Some traditional West Africans also desired to quench their thirst for world domination, but Europeans did not share their privilege. They merely created a sociological space (e.g., slavery) in which blacks could contend for positioning in their own sub-world. The house slave developed the habit of disassociating from the experience of the field slave; the field slave did likewise, and the result of this experience has survived up to the twenty-first century. If African Americans are to embrace fully the Kingian notion of the *Promised Land*, a great deal of work must be done to remedy the negative experience of black privilege. I believe that the civil rights movement, although flawed on many levels, was ultimately successful because blacks from all areas of life used their privilege for good—social integration. Now, in the age of Trumpism, blacks must again become aware of God's movement in history, and forge a bond of togetherness that will not

---

6. Ibid.
7. Graham, *Our Kind of People*, 2.
8. Ibid, 3.
9 Niebuhr, *Moral Man*, 116.

Epilogue

break under the pressure of white supremacy, nor should they be hindered by blacks who are psychologically removed from the experience of *blackness* in America.

Although he, himself, was privileged, Dr. King was willing to suffer and sacrifice in order to create spaces of opportunity for the underprivileged of society. The twenty-first century preacher must embody this type of sacrificial persona. Systemic practices of racism do not *diminish quietly into the night*—such systems tend to persist even in the event of protest. I liken such an experience as a war of attrition. King understood this point quite well, but he also believed that if people are willing to endure, *there is no stopping point short of victory.*

It is illogical to suggest that every white person is bad. Equally illogical is the argument that all black people are good, and that they hold the furtherance of the race as a top priority in life. This, of course, is asinine thinking. There were white people who died during the civil rights movement, and there were some blacks who refused to associate with disorderly [Negros]. Not every black person, in Du Boisian fashion, is *willing* to embrace the notion of community uplift. But for those that desire to change the world, such persons need to understand that privilege is not a bad commodity, in and of itself, to possess. One should obtain as much privilege as possible; it is needed, but it must be used for good. Because this fight regarding the uplift of the black race will be fought on two fronts: against both white and black privileged demagogues.

Bibliography

Adams, E. C. L. *Nigger to Nigger*. New York: Scribner, 1928.
Alexander, Jeffrey C. *Trauma: A Social Theory*. Cambridge: Polity, 2012.
Anderson, Victor. *Creative Exchange: A Constructive Theology of African American Religious Experience*. Minneapolis: Fortress, 2008.
Ansbro, John J. *Martin Luther King, Jr.: Nonviolent Strategies and Tactics for Social Change*. Missoula, MT: Madison, 2000.
Baldwin, Lewis V. "Culture as an Aspect of Black History: An Essay on Slave Culture." PhD diss., Northwestern University, 1976.
———. *Never to Leave Us Alone: The Prayer Life of Martin Luther King Jr*. Minneapolis: Fortress, 2010.
———. *There Is a Balm in Gilead: The Cultural Roots of Martin Luther King, Jr*. Minneapolis: Fortress, 1991.
———. *Toward the Beloved Community: Martin Luther King, Jr. and South Africa*. Cleveland: Pilgrim, 1995.
———. *The Voice of Conscience: the Church in the Mind of Martin Luther King, Jr*. New York: Oxford University Press, 2011.
Baldwin, Lewis V., and Amiri YaSin Al-Hadid. *Between Cross and Crescent: Christian and Muslim Perspectives on Malcolm and Martin*. Gainesville: University Press of Florida, 2002.
Barrett, Leonard E. *Soul-Force: African Heritage in Afro-American Religion*. C. Eric Lincoln Series in Black religion. Garden City, NY: Anchor, 1974.
Barthes, Roland. *Mythologies*. New York: Hill & Wang, 2012.
Battle, Michael. *Reconciliation: The Theology of Desmond Tutu*. Cleveland: Pilgrim, 1997.
Berger, Peter L. *The Sacred Canopy: Elements of a Sociological Theory of Religion*. New York: Doubleday, 1967.
Berlin, Adele, and Marc Zvi Brettler, eds. *The Jewish Study Bible*. Oxford: Oxford University Press, 2014.
Berlin, Ira. *The Making of African America: The Four Great Migrations*. New York: Viking, 2010.
Berry, John W., et al. *Cross-Cultural Psychology: Research and Applications*. 2nd ed. Cambridge: Cambridge University Press, 2008.
Birt, Robert. "Existence, Identity, and Liberation." In *Existence in Black: An Anthology of Black Existential Philosophy*, edited by Lewis R. Gordon, 205–13. New York: Routledge, 1997.

Bibliography

Blassingame, John, ed. *The Slave Community: Plantation Life in the Antebellum South.* New York: Oxford University Press, 1979.

———. *Slave Testimony: Two Centuries of Letters, Speeches, Interviews, and Autobiographies.* Baton Rouge: Louisiana State University Press, 1977.

Brawley, Benjamin G. *A Social History of the American Negro.* New York: Cosimo, 2005.

Brockelman, Paul T. *Existential Phenomenology and the World of Ordinary Experience: An Introduction.* Lanham, MD: University Press of America, 1980.

Brown, Sterling A. "Negro Folk Expression." *Phylon* 11/4 (1950) 320.

Bryan, Andrew. "A Letter From the Negro Baptist Church in Savannah, Addressed to the Reverend Doctor Rippon." In *African American Religious History: A Documentary Witness*, edited by Milton C. Sernett, 49–51. Durham: Duke University Press, 1999.

Callahan, Allen Dwight. *The Talking Book: African Americans and the Bible.* New Haven: Yale University Press, 2006.

Columbus, Christopher. "Christopher Columbus Reports His First Impressions of America: A Letter to Gabriel Sanchez, Treasurer of King Ferdinand of Spain." In *The World's Great Letters*, edited by M. Lincoln Shuster, 61–68. New York: Simon & Schuster, 1940.

Cone, James H. *The Spirituals and the Blues: An Interpretation.* Maryknoll, NY: Orbis, 2003.

Courlander, Harold. *Negro Folk Music, USA.* New York: Columbia University Press, 1963.

Chireau, Yvonne P. *Black Magic: Religion and the African American Conjuring Tradition.* Berkeley: University of California Press, 2003.

Davidson, Basil. *The African Slave Trade.* Boston: Little, Brown, 1980.

———. *The Growth of African Civilisation: A History of West Africa 1000–1800.* London: Longmans, Green, 1967.

Davis, David Brion. *The Problem of Slavery in the Age of Revolution: 1770–1823.* Oxford: Oxford University Press, 1999.

DeGruy, Joy. *Post Traumatic Slave Syndrome: America's Legacy of Enduring Injury and Healing.* 2005. Reprint, Joy DeGruy, 2012.

Derrida, Jacques. *The Animal That Therefore I Am.* Edited by Marie-Louise Mallet. Translated by David Wills. Perspectives in Continental Philosophy. New York: Fordham University Press, 2008.

Diouf, Sylviane A., ed. *Fighting the Slave Trade: West African Strategies.* Athens, OH: Ohio University Press, 2003.

Donne, John. *Select Poems.* Birmingham, AL: Cliff Road, 2007.

Douglas, Kelly Brown. *The Black Christ.* The Bishop Henry McNeal Turner Studies in North American Black Religion 9. Maryknoll, NY: Orbis, 1994.

Du Bois, W. E. B. "Agitation." In *Du Bois: Writings*, edited by Nathan Huggins, 1131–32. New York: Literary Classics of the United States, 1986.

———. *Black Reconstruction in America: 1860–1880.* New York: The Free Press, 1962.

———. "Dusk of Dawn." In *Du Bois: Writings*, edited by Nathan Huggins, 556–57. New York: Literary Classics of the United States, 1986.

———. *The Negro.* New York: Cosimo, 2007.

———. *The Negro Church.* Atlanta: Atlanta University Press, 1903.

———. *Papers (MS 312).* Amherst: University of Massachusetts, 1917.

———. *The Philadelphia Negro: A Social Study.* Philadelphia: University of Pennsylvania, 1996.

Bibliography

———. *Prayers for Dark People.* Edited by Herbert Aptheker. Amherst: The University of Massachusetts, 1980.

———. *The Souls of Black Folk.* Nashville: The Fisk University, 1903. Reprint, 1979.

———. "The Souls of White Folk." In *Du Bois: Writings,* edited by Nathan Huggins, 923–38. New York: Literary Classics of the United States, 1986.

———. "The Study of the Negro Problems." *Annals of the American Academy of Political and Social Science* (January 1898) 1–23.

———. "The Suppression of the African Slave Trade." In *Du Bois: Writings,* edited by Nathan Huggins, 3–356. New York: Literary Classics of the United States, 1986.

———. *The World and Africa: An Inquiry into the Part Which Africa Has Played in World History.* New York: International, 1965.

Dussel, Enrique. "Eurocentrism and Modernity." *Boundary 2* 20/3 (1993) 65–76.

Dyson, Michael Eric. *I May not Get There with You.* New York: Touchstone, 2000.

Earl, Riggins R., Jr. *Dark Symbols, Obscure Signs: God, Self, and Community in the Slave Mind.* Bishop Henry McNeal Turner Studies in North American Black Religion 7. Maryknoll, NY: Orbis, 1993.

Earle, William. *The Autobiographical Consciousness: A Philosophical Inquiry into Existence.* Chicago: Quadrangle, 1972.

Eliade, Mircea. *The Sacred and the Profane: The Nature of Religion.* Translated by Willard R. Trask. New York: Harcourt, Brace & World, 1959.

Elkins, Stanley M. *Slavery.* Chicago: The University of Chicago Press, 1976.

Equiano, Olaudah. "The Interesting Narrative of the Life of Olaudah Equiano, or Gustavus Vassa, The African, Written by Himself." In *The Classic Slave Narratives,* edited by Henry Louis Gates Jr., 17–247. New York: Signet, 1987.

Evans, Curtis. "W. E. B. Du Bois: Interpreting Religion and the Problem of the Negro Church." *Journal of the American Academy of Religion* 75 (2007) 270.

Fanon, Frantz. *The Wretched of the Earth.* Translated by Constance Farrington. New York: Grove, 1963.

Faulkner, William J. *The Days When the Animals Talked.* Trenton, NJ: Africa World, 1993.

Fauset, Arthur Huff. "American Negro Folk Literature." In *The New Negro,* edited by Alain Locke, 248–49. New York: Simon & Schuster, 1992.

Frankl, Viktor E. *Man's Search for Meaning.* New York: Washington Square, 1984.

Franklin, John Hope, and Alfred A. Moss. *From Slavery to Freedom: A History of American Negroes.* 8th ed. New York: Knopf, 2000.

Franklin, John Hope, and Loren Schweninger. *Runaway Slaves: Rebels on the Plantation.* Oxford: Oxford University Press, 1999.

Franklin, Robert Michael. *Liberating Visions: Human Fulfillment and Social Justice in African-American Thought.* Minneapolis: Fortress, 1990.

Frazier, E. Franklin. *The Negro Church in America.* Sourcebooks in Negro History. New York: Schocken, 1963.

———. *The Negro Family in America.* Studies in Sociology. Chicago: University of Chicago Press, 1939.

Frey, Sylvia R., and Betty Wood. *Come Shouting to Zion: African American Protestantism in the American South and British Caribbean to 1830.* Chapel Hill: University of North Carolina Press, 1998.

Gates, Henry Louis, Jr., and Cornel West. *The Future of the Race.* New York: Knopf, 1996.

Genovese, Eugene D. *Roll, Jordan, Roll: The World the Slaves Made.* New York: Pantheon, 1974.

Bibliography

Gerbner, Katherine Reid. "Christian Slavery: Protestant Missions and Slave Conversion in the Atlantic World, 1660-1760." PhD diss., Harvard University, 2013.

Gibran, Kahlil. *The Prophet*. New York: Knopf, 1972.

Gordon, Lewis R. "Du Bois's Humanistic Philosophy of Human Sciences." *Annals of the American Academy of Political and Social Science* 568 (2000) 265–80.

Graham, Lawrence. *Our Kind of People: Inside America's Black Upper Class*. New York: HarperPerennial, 2000.

Grills, Cheryl Tawede. "African Psychology." In *Black Psychology*, edited by Reginald L. Jones, 195. Hampton, VA: Cobb & Henry, 2004.

Guild, June Purcell. *Black Laws of Virginia: A Summary of the Legislative Acts of Virginia Concerning Negroes from Earliest Times to the Present*. 1936. Reprint, New York: Negro Universities, 1969.

Gutman, Herbert. *The Black Family in Slavery and Freedom: 1750–1925*. New York: Vintage, 1976.

Haley, Alex. *Roots: The Saga of an American Family*. New York: Doubleday, 1976.

Hamilton, Charles V. *The Black Preacher in America*. New York: Morrow, 1972.

Hammon, Jupiter. "Address to the Negroes in the State of New York." In *African American Religious History: A Documentary Witness*, edited by Milton C. Sernett, 34–43. Durham: Duke University Press, 1999.

Harding, Vincent. *There Is a River: The Black Struggle for Freedom in America*. New York: Harcourt Brace Jovanovich, 1981.

Harrison, W. P. *Gospel among the Slaves: A Short Account of Missionary Operations among the African Slaves of the Southern States*. Nashville: M.E. Church, 1893.

Hicks, H. Beecher. *Images of the Black Preacher: The Man Nobody Knows*. Valley Forge, PA: Judson, 1977.

Higginson, Thomas Wentworth. "Slave Songs and Spirituals." In *African American Religious History*, edited by Milton C. Sernett, 112–35. Durham: Duke University Press, 1999.

Herman, Judith. *Trauma and Recovery*. New York: Basic Books, 1997.

Holloway, Joseph E. "The Origins of African-American Culture." In *Africanisms in American Culture*, edited by Joseph E. Holloway, 1–18. Blacks in the Diaspora. Bloomington: Indiana University Press, 1990.

Horne, Gerald. *Black and Red: W. E. B. Du Bois and the Afro-American Response to the Cold War, 1944–1963*. Albany: State University of New York Press, 1986.

Hurston, Zora Neale. *Barracoon: The Story of the Last "Black Cargo."* Edited by Deborah G. Plant. New York: Amistad, 2018.

James, William. *Pragmatism*. Buffalo, NY: Prometheus, 1991.

―――. *The Varieties of Religious Experience*. Gifford Lectures 1901–1902. 1902. Reprint, New York: Penguin, 1982.

Jenkins, William Sumner. *Pro-Slavery Thought in the Old South*. Chapel Hill: The University of North Carolina Press, 1935.

Johnson, Clifton H., ed. *God Struck Me Dead: Voices of Ex-Slaves*. Eugene, OR: Wipf & Stock, 2010.

Johnson, Guy. *Drums and Shadows: Survival Studies Amongst the Georgia Coastal Negroes*. Athens: University of Georgia Press, 1940.

Johnson, James Weldon. *God's Trombones: Seven Negro Sermons in Verse*. 1927. Reprint, New York: Penguin, 1990.

Bibliography

Johnson, Shontavia. "Branded: Trademark Tattoos, Slave Owner Brands, and The Right to Have 'Free' Skin." *Michigan Telecommunication and Technology Law Review* 22 (2016) 231. http://repository.law.umich.edu/mttlr/vol22/iss2/2.

Jones, Charles C. *The Religious Instruction of the Negroes in the United States*. Savannah: Thomas Purse, 1842.

Jones, Serene. *Trauma and Grace: Theology in a Ruptured World*. Louisville: Westminster John Knox, 2009.

Jung, C. G. *The Archetypes and the Collective Unconsciousness*. Princeton: Princeton University Press, 1980.

———. *Modern Man in Search of a Soul*. New York: Harcourt, Brace & World, 1933.

Jung, Hwa Yol, ed. *Existential Phenomenology and Political Theory: A Reader*. Chicago: Henry Regnery, 1972.

Kealing, H. T. "The Colored Ministers of the South—Their Preaching and Peculiarities." *The African Methodist Episcopal Church Review* 1/4 (1884) 139–44.

Kelly, Sister. "Proud of That 'Ole Time' Religion." In *African American Religious History: A Documentary Witness*, edited by Milton C. Sernett, 69–75. Durham: Duke University Press, 1999.

Kelly Miller Smith Institute, Inc. "What Does It Mean to Be Black and Christian?" In *Black Theology: A Documentary History*, edited by James H. Cone and Gayraud S. Wilmore, 2:160–74. Maryknoll, NY: Orbis, 1993.

King, Martin Luther. *The Autobiography of Martin Luther King, Jr.* Edited by Clayborne Carson. New York: Warner, 1998.

———. "Beyond Vietnam: A Time to Break Silence." In *The Radical King*, edited by Cornel West, 201–17. Boston: Beacon, 2015.

———. "The Casualties of the War in Vietnam." In *A Time to Break Silence*, edited by Walter Dean Myers, 99–112. Boston: Beacon, 1994.

———. "Christianity and African Religions." In *A Single Garment of Destiny*, edited by Lewis V. Baldwin, 196. Boston: Beacon, 2012.

———. "Drum Major Instinct." In *The Radical King*, edited by Cornel West, 253–64. Boston: Beacon, 2015.

———. "Honoring Dr. Du Bois." In *The Radical King*, edited by Cornel West, 113–21. Boston: Beacon, 2015.

———. "I've Been to the Mountain Top." In *The Radical King*, edited by Cornel West, 265–75. Boston: Beacon, 2015.

———. *The Papers of Martin Luther King, Jr.* Vol. 1, *Called to Serve, January 1929–June 1951*. Edited by Clayborne Carson et al. Berkeley: University of California Press, 1992.

———. *The Papers of Martin Luther King, Jr.* Vol. 4, *Symbol of the Movement, January 1957–December 1958*. Edited by Clayborne Carson et al. Berkeley: University of California Press, 2000.

———. *The Papers of Martin Luther King, Jr.* Vol. 6, *Advocate of the Social Gospel, September 1948–March 1963*. Berkeley: University of California Press, 2007.

———. *The Papers of Martin Luther King, Jr.* Vol. 7, *To Save the Soul of America, January 1961–August 1962*. Edited by Clayborne Carson et al. Berkeley: University of California Press, 2014.

———. "Stride toward Freedom." In *A Testament of Hope: The Essential Writings of Martin Luther King, Jr.*, edited by James Melvin Washington, 417–89. San Francisco: Harper & Row, 1986.

Bibliography

———. "Why Jesus Called a Man a Fool." https://kinginstitute.stanford.edu/king-papers/documents/why-jesus-called-man-fool-sermon-delivered-mount-pisgah-missionary-baptisthttp://kinginstitue.stanford.edu/king-papers/documents/why-jesus-called-man-fool-sermon-delivered-mount-pisgah-missionary-baptist.

———. *Why We Can't Wait*. New York: Harper & Row, 1963.

Klein, Herbert S., et al. "Transoceanic Mortality: The Slave Trade in Comparative Perspective." *William & Mary Quarterly* 58/1 (2001) 93–118.

Lambert, Frank. "'I Saw the Book Talk': Slave Readings of the First Great Awakening." *The Journal of African American History* 87/1 (2002) 12–25.

Lange, Werner J. "W. E. B. Du Bois and the First Scientific Study of Afro-America." *Phylon* 44/2 (1983) 135–46.

Latourette, Kenneth S. *A History of Christianity*. Vol. 1, *Beginnings to 1500*. New York: Harper & Row, 1975.

Lee, Hak Joon. *We Will Get to the Promised Land: Martin Luther King, Jr.'s Communal-Political Spirituality*. Eugene, OR: Wipf & Stock, 2006.

Levine, Lawrence. *Black Culture and Black Consciousness*. Oxford: Oxford University Press, 2006.

Levine, Peter A. *Trauma and Memory: Brain and Body in a Search for the Living Past*. Berkeley: North Atlantic, 2015.

Lewis, David Levering. *W. E. B. Du Bois: Biography of Race*. New York: Holt, 1993.

Long, Charles H. *Significations: Signs, Symbols, and Images in the Interpretation of Religion*. Aurora, CO: The Davies Group, 1995.

Lystad, Robert A. *The Ashanti: A Proud People*. Westport, CT: Greenwood, 1958.

Malraux, André. *The Voices of Silence*. Translated by Stuart Gilbert. 1953. Reprint, New York: Doubleday, 1959.

Marable, Manning. *W. E. B. Du Bois: Black Radical Democrat*. Boulder, CO: Paradigm, 1986.

Marbury, Herbert Robinson. *Pillars of Cloud and Fire*. New York: New York University Press, 2015.

Mather, Cotton. *Magnalia Christi Americana*. http://nationalhumanitiescenter.org/pds/amerbegin/permanence/text3/MatherNewEngland.pdf

Mathews, Donald G. *Religion in the Old South*. Chicago History of American Religion. Chicago: Uni-versity of Chicago Press, 1977.

Matthews, Donald H. *Honoring the Ancestors: An African Cultural Interpretation of Black Religion and Literature*. New York: Oxford University Press, 1998.

Mbiti, John S. *African Religions and Philosophy*. London: Heinemann, 1969.

———. *Introduction to African Religion*. Boston: McGraw-Hill, 2000.

McIntosh, Peggy. *White Privilege and Male Privilege: A Personal Account of Coming to See Correspondences Through Work in Women's Studies*. Wellesley College, Center for Research on Women. 1988.

McKinney, Don S. "Brer Rabbit and Brother Martin Luther King, Jr.: The Folktale Background of the Birmingham Protest." *Journal of Religious Thought* (1975) 42–53.

Merleau-Ponty, Maurice. "Freedom." In *Existential Phenomenology and Political Theory: A Reader*, edited by Hwa Yol Jung, 233–64. Chicago: Regnery, 1972.

Miller, Keith D. *Voice of Deliverance: The Language of Martin Luther King, Jr. and Its Sources*. 1992. Reprint, Athens: University of Georgia Press, 1998.

Mitchell, Henry H. *Black Church Beginnings: The Long-Hidden Realities of the First Years*. Grand Rapids: Eerdmans, 2004.

Bibliography

———. *Black Preaching: The Recovery of a Powerful Art.* Nashville: Abingdon, 1990.
Moustakas, Carl. *Phenomenological Research Methods.* London: Sage, 1994.
Mullane, Deidre, ed. *Crossing the Danger Water.* New York: Doubleday, 1993.
Niebuhr, Reinhold. *Moral Man and Immoral Society: A Study in Ethics and Politics.* Louisville: Westminster John Knox, 1960.
Nunn, Nathan. "The Long-Term Effects of Africa's Slave Trades." *The Quarterly Journal of Economics* 123 (2008) 139–76.
Olmstead, Frederick L. *A Journey in the Back Country.* New York: Franklin, 1970.
O'Loughlin, Michael, and Marilyn Charles, eds. *Fragments of Trauma and the Social Production of Suffering: Trauma, History, and Memory.* New York: Rowan & Littlefield, 2015.
Paris, Peter J. *Virtues and Values: The African and African American Experience. Facets.* Minneapolis: Fortress, 2004.
———. *The Spirituality of African Peoples: The Search for a Common Moral Discourse.* Minneapolis: Fortress, 1995.
Parrinder, Geoffrey. *African Mythology.* London: Hamlyn, 1967.
———. *Religion in Africa.* Baltimore: Penguin, 1969.
Patterson, Orlando. *Slavery and Social Death: A Comparative Study.* Cambridge: Harvard University Press, 1982.
Pinn, Anthony. *Terror and Triumph: The Nature of Black Religion.* Minneapolis: Fortress, 2003.
Pipes, William H. *Say Amen, Brother! Old-Time Negro Preaching.* Detroit: Wayne State University Press, 1951.
Puckett, Newbell Niles. *Folk Beliefs of the Southern Negro.* Chapel Hill: University of North Carolina, 1926.
Raboteau, Albert J. *Canaan Land: The Religious History of African Americans.* Oxford: Oxford University Press, 1999.
———. "Introduction." In *God Struck Me Dead: Voices of Ex-Slaves,* edited by Clifton H. Johnson, x–xxv. Eugene, OR: Wipf & Stock, 2010.
———. *Slave Religion: The "Invisible Institution" in the Antebellum South.* Oxford: Oxford University Press, 1978.
Radin, Paul. "Foreword." In *God Struck Me Dead: Voices of Ex-Slaves,* edited by Clifton H. Johnson, viii–ix. Eugene, OR: Wipf & Stock, 2010.
Rampersad, Arnold. *The Art and Imagination of W. E. B. Du Bois.* New York: Schocken, 1990.
Raper, Arthur. *The Tragedy of Lynching.* Chapel Hill: The University of North Carolina Press, 1933.
Rawick, George, ed. *The American Slave: A Composite Autobiography.* 41 vols. Westport, CT: Greenwood, 1941.
Rodney, Walter. *How Europe Underdeveloped Africa.* New Jersey: African Tree, 2014.
Salzberger, Ronald P., and Mary Turck. *Reparations for Slavery.* Lanham, MD: Rowan & Littlefield, 2004.
Simmons, Martha. "Whooping: The Musicality of African American Preaching Past and Present." In *Preaching With Sacred Fire: An Anthology of African American Sermons, 1750 to the Present,* edited by Martha Simmons and Frank A. Thomas, 865–84. New York: Norton, 2010.

Bibliography

Shanks, Caroline L. "The Biblical Anti-Slavery Argument of the Decade 1830–1840." In *Biblical Studies Alternatively: An Introductory Reader*, edited by Susanne Scholz, 203–16. Upper Saddle River, NJ: Prentice Hall, 2003.

Sloat, William A. "George Whitefield, African-Americans, and Slavery." *Methodist History* 33/1 (1994) 3–13.

Smith, Kenneth L. *Search for the Beloved Community: The Thinking of Martin Luther King, Jr.* Valley Forge, PA: Judson, 1974.

Sobel, Mechal. *Teach Me Dreams: Transforming the Self in the Revolutionary Era.* Princeton: Princeton University Press, 2000.

———. *Trabelin' On: The Slave Journey to an Afro-Baptist Faith.* Contributions in Afro-American and African Studies 36. Westport, CT: Greenwood, 1979.

Stallworth, DeWayne. *Stable Conscience: Awareness of God, Self, and Others.* Nashville: True Vine, 2013.

Stamp, Kenneth M. *The Peculiar Institution.* New York: Vintage, 1989.

Stroyer, Jacob. *My Life in the South.* Salem, MA: Newcomb & Gauss, 1898.

Stuckey, Sterling. *Slave Culture: Nationalist Theory and the Foundations of Black America.* Oxford: Oxford University Press, 1988.

Sweet, James H. *Recreating Africa: Culture, Kinship, and Religion in the African-Portuguese World, 1441–1770.* Chapel Hill: University of North Carolina Press, 2003.

Tamez, Elsa. "The Bible and Five Hundred Years of Conquest." In *Voices from the Margin: Interpreting the Bible in the Third World*, edited by R. S. Sugirtharajah, 3–18. Maryknoll, NY: Orbis, 2006.

Thurman, Howard. *Jesus and the Disinherited.* New York: Abingdon-Cokesbury, 1949.

Todorov, Tzvetan, *The Conquest of America: The Question of the Other.* Norman: University of Oklahoma Press, 1999.

Touchstone, Blake. "Planters and Slave Religion in the Deep South." In *Masters and Slaves in the House of the Lord: Race and Religion in the American South, 1740–1870*, edited by John B. Boles, 99–126. Lexington: University of Kentucky Press, 1990.

Van der Kolk, Bessel A. *The Body Keeps Score: Brain, Mind, and Body in the Healing of Trauma.* New York: Penguin, 2014.

Van Der Leeuw, G. *Religion in Essence and Manifestation.* Translated by J. E. Turner. New York: Harper & Row, 1963.

Washington, Joseph R. *Black Sects and Cults.* C. Eric Lincoln Series on Black religion. New York: Doubleday, 1972.

Wells, H. G. *The Outline of History.* Vol. 2. New York: Doubleday, 1961.

Wells-Barnett, Ida B. *On Lynchings.* Mineola, NY: Dover, 2014.

West, Cornel. *The American Evasion of Philosophy: A Genealogy of Pragmatism.* Madison: University of Wisconsin Press, 1989.

Whatley, William D. *Roots of Resistance.* Valley Forge, PA: Judson, 1985.

Wheatley, Phyllis. "On Being Brought From Africa to America." In *Crossing the Danger Water: Three Hundred Years of African-American Writing*, edited by Deirdre Mullane, 41. New York: Doubleday, 1993.

White, William S. *The African Preacher: An Authentic Narrative.* London: Forgotten, 2015.

Whitefield, George. *George Whitefield Journals.* Carlisle, PA: Banner of Truth Trust, 1960.

———. "What Think Ye of Christ?" In *Sermons of George Whitefield*, edited by Evelyn Bence, 9783–98. Peabody, MA: Hendrickson, 2009.

Wilken, Robert L. *The First Thousand Years: A Global History of Christianity.* New Haven: Yale University Press, 2012.

Bibliography

William, George W. *History of the Negro Race in America from 1619 to 1880*. New York: Firework, 2015.

Wilmore, Gayraud S. *Black Religion and Black Radicalism: An Interpretation of the Religious History of African Americans*. New York: Anchor, 1973.

Wilson, Monica. *Rituals of Kinship among the Nyakyusa*. London: Oxford University Press, 1957.

Woodson, Carter G., ed. *The Mind of the Negro: As Reflected in Letters during the Crisis 1800–1860*. Mineola, NY: Dover, 2013.

———. *The Negro in Our History*. Washington, DC: Associated Publishers, 1922.

Yehuda, Rachel et al. "Holocaust Exposure Induced Intergenerational Effects on FKBP5 Methylation." *Society of Biological Psychiatry* 80 (September 2016) 372–80

Yetman, Norman R. ed. *Voices from Slavery*. New York: Holt, Rinehart, and Winston, 1970.

Zinn, Howard. *A People's History of the United States*. New York: HarperCollins, 1980.

Index

abolitionists, 8
acculturated slaves, 29, 30, 40
   accustomed, 29
African American religious
      experience, xv, xviii
   African priest, 72, 74
   American community, xx
   ancestral spirits, 23
   antislavery advocates, 4
   communal identity, 30
   consciousness, 66
   cosmology, xix, 58, 100
   cultural roots, 71
   existential meaning, 13
   faith tradition, 19
   familial patterns, 10
   folklore, 85
   heritage, 30, 43, 70, 131
   mythology, xix, 79
   privilege, 140
      black, xx, 56, 138–39
   psyche, 1, 18, 43, 53, 92
   religious hermeneutic, 42
   ring shout, 132
   togetherness, 25, 29
   traditions, 111–14
agape, 106–8, 119
agitation, 108, 134
Akan, 13, 58
Alexander, Jeffery C., 64
American cultural variations, 43
American pharaoh, 49
amistad mutiny, 30
Anderson, Victor, 133

"apollonian myth," 134
Ashanti, 19, 73
"axis mundi," 32
Aztecs, 37, 40

Balaam, Chilam, 42
Baldwin, Lewis V., 99, 111, 116
Ball, Charles, 44
Bakongo, 13
baracoons, 5, 131
Barrett, Leonard E., vii, 11, 73
Babylonian, 67
beloved community, 134
Bennett, Lerone, 11
Berlin, Ira, 59
Bibb, Henry, 55
biblical parallelism, 106
Birmingham campaign, 132
black culture, 99
   aristocracy, 137
   black folk, 10
   black life, 98, 131, 140
   black radicalism, 128
   church, xviii, 52, 95, 111–13, 129, 132–34
   discontinuity, xx
   faith, 113
   liberative hermeneutic, 50
   liberation, 108
   intelligentsia, 96
   masses, 120
   psyche, 46, 50, 107
   preachers, 52–54, 87, 104, 114, 129

Index

black culture (*continued*)
    preaching tradition, 114
    religion, 92, 103
    religious community, 100
    social consciousness, 111, 123
        group sub-consciousness, 138
Blassingame, John, 11, 45, 54–56, 65, 67–68
    shock of middle passage, 71–72
Brawley, Benjamin, 10, 69
Bray, Thomas, 76
brer rabbit, 83–85
Brightman, Edgar S, 117
Brooks, Phillip, 114
Bryan, Andrew, 4–5
Buttrick, George, 114
Buxton, Thomas Fowell, 6

capitalism, 57
Carson, Clayborne, 109
catechism, 76
Chamberlain, Alexander Francis, 10
chattel slavery, 16–18, 26, 44, 60, 71
Christianity
    missions, 614
    Society for the Propagation of the Gospel, 76
    white, 40
    white Christ, 47
    white religion, 92
civil rights era, 11
    movement, 92, 101, 128–29, 131–32, 135, 140
clan, 18
community, xviii, xix 13, 22–23, 26–28
    communal heritage, xvii
    common religious heritage, xviii, 15, 18, 132
    communal religious politic, 134
    communal survival, 18
collective unconsciousness, 46
Columbus, Christopher, 36–39, 42
conversion, 74, 76
Cortes, Hernando, 37–39
cosmology, 13, 80
    cosmic companion, 116, 126

cosmic shift, 66
cosmological collision, 57
cultural memory, 71
cultural theory, 56n
cultural transmissions, 111
cultural trauma, 61
cultural variations, 38
crisis moment, 115–16
Cuffy, 73

Davidson, Basil, 18, 20
Davis, David Brion, 2
Davis, George, 128, 114, 117
"death march," 69
deceiver, 91
deception, 83
"Declaration of Independence," 40
Dexter Avenue Baptist Church, 104
De Gruy, Joy, 64
dehumanization, 10, 26, 58, 67
demagogues, 141
dialectical tension, 100
diaspora, 22
divine, 20, 122
    privilege, 31
DNA, 70
    transgenerational epigenetic inheritance, 70
Donne, John, 40
Douglas, Kelly Brown, 47
drums, 15, 81, 90
Dr. Watts hymn, 89
Du Bois, W. E. B., xix, 5, 9–10, 25, 53, 72, 92–95, 97, 99–100, 104, 108, 114, 137
    Grand Boule`, 96
    new world, 96
    participant-observer, 97
    Philadelphia Negro, 10n
    talented tenth, 95
    "willing spirit," 96
    double consciousness, 10, 93
Dyson, Michael Eric, 120

Earl, Riggins, xvi
Earle, William, xvii

Index

Egyptians, 50
  Egypt, 88
Elijah and Elisha, 101
Elkins, Stanley, 67–69, 71
emancipation, 26, 53
enslaved Africans, 47
essence, xvi, xvii, 4, 12, 22
Equiano, Olaudah, 20
existential
  burdens, 121
  concern, 118
  crisis, 57–58, 91
  freedom, 128
  isolation, 51, 120
  meaning, 66
  meaninglessness, 5, 44
  philosophers, 121
  phenomenology, xvi
  responsibility, 96
  togetherness, xv, xviii, xix, 6n, 18, 24, 30, 104, 113, 120, 126, 130, 137–38
Exodus narrative, 49
European institution of slavery, 14
Evangelical liberalism, 128

familial hereditary, 72
Fanon, Frantz, 31
Fausett, Arthur Huff, 85
Federal Bureau of Investigation, 122
Ferdinand of Aragon, 36
feudalism, xix, 57
First Great Awakening, 61, 76
folktales, 81
Franklin, Robert Michael, 100
Frankl, Viktor, 73
Franklin, John Hope, 11
Francisco, J. T., 104
Frazier, E. Franklin, 10, 51
  "Great Debate," 98
Fulani, 83

Graham, Lawrence Otis, 140
Gutman, Herbert, 12

Hamilton, Charles, 54
Harding, Vincent, 12

Hausa, 83
heritage, 108
Herman, Judith, 63
heroic symbol, 134
Herskovits, Melville, 11
Heschel, Abraham, 121
Hicks, H Beecher, 54
hip hop culture, 138
Holloway, Joseph, 139
Holocombie, Dr., 4
house slave, 140
Howard, Nancy, 63
human personality, 37, 130
Hurston, Zora Neale, 5
hush harbors, 52, 86
Husserl, Edmund, xv
  "things themselves," xvi

Ibo, 13
  traditional, 20
Ignatius, 34
individualism, 131
individuality, 131
ingenuity, xvii, 16, 83, 92
institution of slavery, 2, 3
invisible institution, 51
Isabella of Castile, 36
Israelites, 67

Jenkins, William Sumner, 3
Jewish holocaust victims, 68
  concentration camps, 68
Johnson, James Weldon, 61
Jones, C. C., 4
Jung, C. G., 46, 65

Kassongo, 5
Kealing, H. T., 53
Kendall, Hiram, 118
kinship, 18, 19
king buzzard, 82–83
King, Martin Luther, xx, 54, 92
  African religious tradition, 112
  black consciousness, 123
  black religion, 103
  co-creators with God, 107
  "Daddy King," 110, 121

Index

King, Martin Luther (*continued*)
   Ebony magazine, 111
   Exodus theme of deliverance, 107
   (and) existential togetherness,
      113, 120, 130, 132, 137
   God of history, 108, 126, 129
   God *in* history, 128
   heroic image, 107
   Kingian church model, 124
   Lorraine Hotel, 104, 122
   nonviolent direct action, 91, 108
   privileged tradition, 103, 120, 121
   relevant ministry, 126, 129
   restorative potentiality, 101
   symbol, 105
   truth, 106
   "willing to sacrifice," 121

Lange, Werner, 94
Lawson, James, 122
Lebenswelt, xv
   everyday life-world, xv, xvii
   lived experience, xvii
legitimate priests
legitimation, 33
   indoctrination of ideals, 35
Levine, Lawrence, 11, 43
Levine, Peter L., 70
Lewis, Cudjo, 6
Lewis, David Levering, 99
liberal evangelicalism, 129
lived experiences, 69, 79
living dead, 68, 69
Locke, Alaine, 10
Long, Charles H, 11
Luthuli, Arthur J, 113

Malcom X, 119
Malfante, Antonio, 2
Mamdu, Lord of Mali, 14
Mandika, 83
manifest destiny, 37, 40
Manning, Patrick, 58
Marbury, Herbert, 107
marcionites, 35
mass incarceration, 134–135
Mather, Cotton, 3, 8

Matthews, Donald, xvi
Mays, Benjamin E., xvi, 10
Mbiti, John, 17, 18, 66
McIntosh, Peggy, 139
McKinney, Don S., 84
meaninglessness, xix, 30
middle passage, 44, 60, 69, 139, 60
Miller, Keith D., 114
Mitchell, Henry T., 72
modernity, xix, 38-39
montanists, 35
Montejo, Esteban, 5
Moses, 107, 120
   comfort, 121
Montgomery Bus Boycott, 116
Muhammed, Hamed, 5
mythology, 79
   myth (s), 63, 80
   "farewell address," 125

NAACP, 107, 110
natural law, 8
Negro church, 9n
new world, xix, xvii, 15, 35, 37, 43,
      60, 70–72
   newly enslaved Africans, 42–43
   trauma, 73
Niebuhr, Reinhold, 140
"nomos" of a society, 33
non-violent direct action, 122
notions of conquest, 36
"nulli secundus," 31
Nyakyusa, 19
obeahman, 73–74
ontological self, 58
oral tradition, 19, 26
   orality, 76
   transmission, 16
otherness
   "other," 37, 39, 40, 74

Paris, Peter, 12, 17, 23, 27, 28, 58
Parks, Rosa, 119–120
Parr, Patrick, 117
Parrinder, Geoffrey, 18, 79, 83
paternalistic theology, 62
peculiar institution, 3, 21, 51

Index

Penn, William, 3
phenomenon, xviii, xix, xx, 12, 51
  individual essences, xv
  lived experience, xvii
  natural, 68
  personalism, 117
    as seen in human personality, 117
  "phaenesthai," xv
  phenomena, 61
  phenomenological manifestations, 31
  pure phenomenology, xv
  sub-world, xv
Pinn, Anthony, 7
"Plessy v. Ferguson," 9
Poor People's Campaign, 122, 127
Poullain, Parker, 109
"pragmatics of slavery," 57
prayer circle, 132
priest, 10n, 26, 80
privilege, xx, 38, 40–41, 56n, 93, 131, 137–38, 141
  African, 140
  blacks, 137
  gendered, 139
  race, 139
  white, xx, 137
  white male, 139
Prince Henry, 34
prophetic tradition of social activism, 135
Prosser, Gabriel, 11
protest, 59, 65, 108
  tradition of black, 15
  reactionary, 134
psyche, 66, 78, 97, 112
  traumatized enslaved, 65
  human, 70
Puritans, 2, 3

Quakers, 3
Queen Nzinga, 14

Raboteau, Albert, 11, 13, 22, 55, 56
race inferiority, 93
Rampersad, Arnold, 98

Reconstruction, 113
religious formalism, 76
Richard, Pablo, 42
Roper, Moses, 55

sacred, 21
sacrifice, 129
sanitation workers, 122
"Sasa," 66
Sernett, Milton, 11
Sewell, Samuel, 3
Sister Kelly, 22
slave community, 55, 56, 61, 62, 73, 86, 87
slave consciousness, 50
slave culture, 83, 117, 130
slave heritage, 140
slave holding Christianity, 48, 50
slave masters, 3, 4, 45, 50, 71
slave preacher, xix, xx, 53, 54, 61, 72, 74, 78–81, 86, 87, 89, 91, 101, 103, 108–10, 129–30
  conversion, 63, 76, 78
  double agent, 62
  genius, 62
  Hammon, Jupiter, 62
  Jasper, John, 89
  manipulator, 56
  parallelism, 88, 130
  parasitic type, 62
  preaching, 135
  privileged, 56
  rhetorical tension, 88
  slave preaching tradition, 134–135
  trouble maker, 54
  Uncle Jack, 56
  unified, 73
slave religion, 44, 46, 95
slave ships, 5, 24, 59, 63, 82, 70, 132
  division, 139
slave spirituals, 26, 27, 28
  slave songs, 98, 131
slave traumatization, 65
Sobel, Mechal, 12
social agitation, 129

Index

social consciousness, 109–10
    "heritage," 110
social privilege, 115
social stratification, 45, 56n
"Somebody-ness," 116
sorcerer, 73
soul equity/equality, 4
space, 52, 94, 95
    sacred, xviii
    sociological, 140
    (s), 112
Stamp, Kenneth M., 12
sub-group, 56n
sub-world, 140
Suffin, John, 3
Supreme God, 81
    Supreme Being, 15, 20–21
suicide, 68
supreme personality, 128
stratification, 139
    "social," 139
Stuckey, Sterling, xvii, 97
survival, 24, 61–62, 73, 83, 91, 131, 134–135
    testimonies, 103
Swahili, 66
Sweet, James H., 65
symbol (s), 80–81, 105
    Moses, 89
    Moses/Jesus like figure, 104

tradition of black protest, 129
trauma, 63–64, 66–69, 71
tribal differences, 24
trickster-transformer hero, 83
theory of slave acquiescence, 11
Thornton, John, 70
Thurman, Howard, 48, 81
Todorov, Tzvetan, 38

Togetherness
    among the enslaved, 16
    human, 22
    notions of, 28
    slaves sang about, 90
Turner, Nat, 11, 108
    survival, 91
    violent direct action, 91
tribe, xviii
    see clan, xvii

ubuntu, 22
unitary consciousness, 58

Van Der Leeuw, G., 79
Vesey, Denmark, 11
victimization, 57

Walker, David, 11
Wallace, Christopher, 138
Washington, Booker T., 109
Washington, James Melvin, 119
Washington, Joseph, 11
Whatley, William, 128
Wheatley, Phyllis, 17
Whitefield, George, 76
Wilkins, Roy, 107
Williams, Adam Daniel (A.D.), 91, 109
Williams, Alberta Christine, 110
Williams, George Washington, 9
Williams, Willis, 91, 108
Wilmore, Gayraud, 61
Wolof Tales, 83
Woodson, Carter G, 10

"Zamani," 66
Zeitgeist, 94, 104, 106

www.ingramcontent.com/pod-product-compliance
Lightning Source LLC
Chambersburg PA
CBHW071458150426
43191CB00008B/1385